Release

Flora Slosson Wuellner

Release

Healing from Wounds of Family,
Church, and Community

UPPER
ROOM BOOKS
NASHVILLE

Release

Unless otherwise noted scripture quotations are from the New Revised Standard Version of the Bible, © 1989 by the Division of Christian Education, National Council of the Churches of Christ in the USA, and are used by permission.

Scripture quotations designated RSV are from the Revised Standard Version of the Bible, copyrighted 1946, 1952, and © 1971 by the Division of Christian Education, National Council of the Churches of Christ in the USA. Used by permission.

Scripture quotations designated TEV are from the *Good News Bible*, The Bible in Today's English Version—Old Testament: Copyright © American Bible Society 1976; New Testament: Copyright © American Bible Society 1966, 1971, 1976.

Prayers from the *Book of Worship, United Church of Christ* Copyright © 1986 United Church of Christ, Office for Church Life and Leadership, New York, NY. Used by permission.

Prayer from "Ministry with Persons Going Through Divorce" from *The United Methodist Book of Worship*. Copyright © 1992 by The United Methodist Publishing House. Used by permission.

Cover photograph: © Garry Blank / Masterfile
Cover design: Jim Bateman
Interior design and typesetting: Nancy Cole

Library of Congress Cataloging-in-Publication Data

Wuellner, Flora Slosson
Release: healing from wounds of family, church, and community /
Flora Slosson Wuellner.
p.   cm.
ISBN 0-8358-0775-4 (pbk.)
1. Spiritual healing. 2. Interpersonal relations—Religious Aspects—Christianity. 3. Prayer—Christianity. 4. Meditations.
I. Title.
BT732.5.W84 1996
234'.13—dc20   95-39580

Printed in the United States of America
First printing: January 1996 (7)

*This book is dedicated with warm appreciation
to the editors and staff of Upper Room Books
who have worked with me for over eleven years,
and from whom I have learned so much.*

Contents

Suggestions for Use of Guided Meditations

There are many suggested guided prayer meditations in this book, most of them based on biblical passages. It is hoped they will be helps along the way in this adventure of release and healing. You are free to enter into these meditations, or to lay them aside. Some will be helpful to you, and you may wish to return to them several times. Others may not be quite what you need.

Most of them are visual meditations, using inner images, pictures, symbols, and metaphors. Some of the suggested inner pictures may not feel helpful. In that case, ask God to give you an inner picture, image, symbol which is better for you.

If you are working as a group leader or a group member, make it clear to yourself and others that each person present is free to make inner changes of the suggested symbols, or is free to withdraw from any of the meditations. The only authority is God through the living Christ within our hearts.

You may discover that visualizing is not a natural or comfortable way for you to pray or meditate. There are always some in each group who feel this way. This is quite natural, and no one should push himself or herself. Move into some other way of praying, such as choosing a meaningful word or phrase which helps you feel God's nearness, and focus on that. Or think about your slow, gentle breathing, knowing each breath is God's breath of life breathed into you. Or think of light or a color and sit quietly soaking in it. The scriptures are full of references to God's light and God's breath. These are powerful ways of praying. Trust yourself and the way God guides *you*.

You may find during your deep meditation that you are

getting in touch with some level of anxiousness or pain which you do not choose to enter at this time. You are free to withdraw from the process at any point. You may wish to discuss your feelings later with the group leader or with a trusted friend. More will be said about this in chapter two as well as further suggestions given for a releasing approach to spiritual healing.

1

Empowered Vulnerability: Love Set Free

I arise today through the strength of heaven:
light of the sun, radiance of moon,
splendor of fire, speed of lightning,
swiftness of wind, depth of sea,
stability of earth, firmness of rock.
I arise today through God's strength to pilot me . . .
God's word to speak for me,
God's hand to guard me,
God's way to lie before me.
I summon all these powers between me and every
  power
that may oppose my body and soul.
                    —attributed to Saint Patrick, 500 AD

The dark wounding through the generations, the toxicity in communities around us, have begun to enter our consciousness in many ways.

We see the ancient inherited shadows between the warring nations and the bitterly embattled great ethnic groups. We see the generational burdens in our families, and the wounds we absorb from one another, the energy drained in our personal relationships.

Is the pain of our communal bodies the new frontier of healing? Can this vast pain that spans decades, even centuries, be healed? Can we personally be healed by God and set free from the burden and the bleeding? How can one pray for inherited and absorbed wounding?

Today I read again a newspaper article I cut out some years ago and kept. It is the writer's own story. He tells how he saw reflected in a subway window his father's expression stamped on his own face: tight, stressed, angry. He recalls how that expression of his father frightened him as a child. His son is also developing that same expression. What is this family wound passed through generations?

There are so many ways by which generational and communal infection can be carried from person to person. Ministers, counselors, caregivers often share with me the drained exhaustion they feel when working with certain people, certain groups. It does not necessarily have any connection with outer demands.

"When I'm counseling with certain people, I feel as if the corks had been pulled out of the bottoms of my feet and my energy drains right down through the floor!" one woman shared with me.

Yet another tells me that when he walks into his office building, he feels a sudden heavy depression, like a dark shadow. Since he took the job he has begun to have unusual bodily symptoms which seem to have no organic cause. This is bewildering, because he likes the work itself, and his colleagues are friendly.

A young woman tells me that outwardly her family is pleasant, respected in the community, but when she attends family reunions she feels trapped, almost as if there were not air enough to breathe. She senses unspoken *neediness* clustering around her. Nothing she is, does, says, is enough for the needs.

Far more than we realize, we inherit emotional burdens, communal darkness, experience heavy draining like a chronic emotional hemorrhaging from our relationships and the groups to which we belong.

Deep communal infection may or may not be connected with outer forms of emotional, verbal, or physical abuse.

It may or may not lead to outer forms of what we call dysfunctional families, churches, workplaces. Yet I am convinced that many of our illnesses, depressions, emotional and bodily symptoms of all sorts are rooted in communal darkness, invasion, draining.

Some years ago a beautiful, gentle older woman came to talk to me. She was struggling with severe illness and loss of vitality. "I have prayed; I have gone through therapy; I have been to healing retreats; I have experienced healing of memories. What am I doing wrong spiritually and emotionally? What mistakes am I making?" Tears were in her eyes as she talked with me.

As far as I could see, she was not doing *anything* wrong. Not only was she allowing her personal wounds to be healed and her prayer life nurtured but she was aware of the need to set limits to her time and energy output. I could not see any aspect of her personal life where she was making wrong choices.

As we talked together she eventually told me, rather casually, that most of her volunteer time was spent working with her church, which was going through severe crisis. She had been a member for several years, and there always seemed to be some uproar or another.

"It's strange." She said thoughtfully, "It was the same in the church before this one, too. Is it possible that I could be 'catching' something like an emotional virus from these groups? I never heard of such a thing."

I had never heard of such a thing either, but it started me thinking. Several similar stories were told me by other people. I began noticing my own symptoms and reactions in certain relationships.

We are all increasingly aware of dangerous levels of toxicity, chemical poisoning in our air, water, food, soil, even in building materials. But only slowly, dimly are we becoming aware of similar toxicity in our emotional surroundings, our relationships, our communities.

I no longer believe that *all* our problems are results of our individual choices and mistakes, or that we as individuals have created all our own reality. In our marriages, friendships, church memberships, professional work, our gender and ethnic groups, our nations, we may have inherited or absorbed dangerous levels of toxicity, communal darkness.

We can become sick with wounds that did not begin with ourselves!

But how do we become aware of this reality? As with environmental toxicity, emotional poisoning may be imperceptible at first. We usually do not realize how overloaded, how saturated we are until symptoms begin to show. We may have breathed emotionally contaminated air all our lives, or for many years, not knowing of other atmospheres. The toxic shadow may have existed for decades in a church, for generations in a family, or for hundreds of years or more in a nation or ethnic group.

This can be a startling and painful, even frightening realization. It goes counter to so much of what we have been taught and what we have expected. There is nothing really new in it. It is a frequent scriptural perception. It is taken for granted in sociological research and in much psychological research that we are communal beings, sharing intimately in the shadow and pain as well as the gifts and powers of our communal bodies. The daily life in many cultures is not centered around individual self-perception at all, but rather on the communal body as a unified whole.

Even in our more individualized cultures we know of and perhaps have experienced "mob spirit," or the curious unified body of fans cheering on a team, or the close communal body of those listening to music, singing, cheering a charismatic politician.

But I think it is a reality we are apt to forget or to deny in our ordinary daily lives when we seem to be living as individuals. We forget, or simply do not know, that even when alone, minding our own business, we are living, moving, and breathing in the needs, projections, pictures, expectations, energy demands, empowered light, and infected shadow of others.

Spiritual leaders like myself have not yet fully perceived this, and most of us have not dealt with either the gifted or the shadow side of this reality in our healing and spiritual renewal movements. It isn't part of our teaching about prayer.

Many questions rise. If we do become aware of the communal sea around us constantly influencing us, whether nurturing or draining, is there anything special we can *do* about it? Do we just accept it as part of our human condition? If we sense in ourselves an infected, poisoned overload, can we be cleansed and healed? If we feel ourselves in some sort of communal trap or prison, can we be set free? What does being set free mean? Does it mean leaving these relationships? Is it our responsibility to stay and help the wounded and wounding communal body? Should we ask for spiritual protection? Does our Christian religion have any light or guidance at this point? Where does prayer come in, if at all?

Perhaps we ask a more troubling question. *Should* Christians ask to be set free from a communal shadow or infection? Aside from the mere acceptance of the human condition, are we not called as Christians to be open to the world's pain and carry the cross of suffering for others? Are we, followers of Christ, to retreat into shells of defensiveness or to mountaintops of detachment?

Often in the past when I have officiated at a Communion service, when I broke the bread I would urge us all to be broken also for others, as nourishment for others. When I would pour and give the cup, I would say that we should pour out ourselves for others. I did not stop to ask myself or others when does breaking become self-shredding? When does pouring become hemorrhaging?

Even if I did become aware that I was shredded and

hemorrhaging, I would usually silence my questions with the assertion that this was the proper condition and stance of a "suffering servant."

But the questions kept rising, particularly with reference to this whole area of woundedness that was so easy to ignore, the unconscious infection, the *unconscious* shadow we have inherited or absorbed, the weights and wounds that did not begin with ourselves and which we had not chosen.

When I read a witness like that of Saint Patrick's prayer which opens this chapter, I was given another picture of the Christian stance. I heard another voice and breathed another air. There is a freedom, a strength, a boldness in this prayer. It is saturated with risk-taking love. It is not the voice of a hermit in a cave, or one walled off from the world's pain. Neither is it the voice of one who is self-shredded or drained to the hemorrhaging point. Somehow it combines the sovereign strength to choose with the sovereign passion of love.

Even more startling and empowered is Jesus, when we read the Gospels as if we had never read them before. Again we breathe another air and see love as a passionate empowered inner flame. It is *not* the stance of victimhood. It is *not* the powerlessness that submits to invasion. Its foundation is not that of unawareness and self-abnegation. Rather, I see love's response flowing out of radiant strength; love's response flowing out of freedom, not bondage.

The good we are to return for evil is not an emotional disempowerment, much less a surrender to evil. It is a power of radical energy and strength.

The cross we are invited to lift and carry has nothing to do with being invaded, overcome, drained. It has nothing to do with carrying burdens without our knowledge and consent. The cross is our free choice and consent to lift in full conscious awareness, knowing what we do, something of the world's pain. It is not the same as being *infected* by another's pain.

When Jesus returned from his desert experience of discernment, he spoke his passionate purpose:

"To bring good news to the poor.
. . . to proclaim release to the captives
and recovery of sight to the blind,
to let the oppressed go free."
— Luke 4:18

Release from every manner of captivity was spoken then and is spoken now to our bodies, minds, hearts, and spirits, both as community and as individuals.

It fascinates me that Jesus put release into instant practice, first for himself, then for others. When the enraged crowd in his own home town of Nazareth tried to execute him for blasphemy by throwing him over a cliff at the very start of his ministry, he *left*. This was not the right time. It was not the right place. It was not the cross that he had chosen.

That very day he left his home and went to other cities preaching release, liberating victims from the power of the demonic, from illness, speaking with the empowered authority of one who could set others free because *he* was set free. And when out of clutching love and need they tried to hold on to him in these other cities, limit his releasing love to themselves only, again he left.

"I must proclaim the good news of the
kingdom of God
to the other cities also;
for I was sent for this purpose."
— Luke 4:43

Love, to him, was never bondage, not for him and not for others. In the midst of healing, comforting, reconciliation, he faced the realities and spoke the hard truths. He did not avoid confrontation. He did not fear his own anger. He recognized and named evil, the demonic, the destructive. When he needed to eat and sleep, he ate and slept. When he needed to be alone, he did not hesitate to leave the crowds for renewal in prayer, and he encouraged his disciples to do the same. When he grieved he cried, and he let himself be touched and comforted by those who loved him.

His *whole* empowered, freely chosen life was his cross. When he chose the final, bodily cross it was the right time and the right place. In the midst of it, though he experienced human fear, he also experienced God's intimate closeness. As he faced arrest, it was not with powerlessness, but with a victor's stance. Brushing away Peter's sword, drawn in his defense, Jesus spoke of the "more than twelve legions of angels" that would come to his defense if he chose (Matt. 26:53). (Incidentally, according to the Roman designation of a *legion*, that would mean 72,000 angels altogether!) This was Jesus' way of saying that the power of the whole of God's universe backed him. He did not need to use physical force. True power is the *opposite* of force.

This is the stance I have begun to call "empowered vulnerability." It means the love that has been set free by God to choose freely, to take risks, to reach out, to withdraw, to suffer, to give from a deep center that has been released from prisons of all kinds, and knows clearly what it does.

When we are moved by love to reach out and rescue another person who is drowning in emotional crisis and anguish, it is a love that does *not* disempower either the rescuer or the rescued.

This released passion of love has nothing to do with self-shredding, or surrender to drowning either for the other *or* for the self. It is the released passion of the rescuer who intends to get the victim and one's self to the shore as soon as possible, to set both upon their own feet. It is *not* the codependency that permits both to go under, or both to remain in an indefinite stranglehold of a rescue operation.

Here are some of the signs of empowered vulnerability:

We are increasingly free in our choices.

We increasingly allow ourselves to be spontaneous in loving and giving.

We become aware of what we really feel, not what we "ought" to feel.

We recognize our limits without guilt or fear.

We know the signs of emotional invasion and bondage.

We are able to see the source and name the problem.

We understand the meaning and need of spiritual protection.

We take time and space for bodily and emotional renewal.

We allow ourselves freedom to explore options and alternatives.

We can enter appropriate confrontation with love and firmness.

We can recognize our *own* cross of loving service.

We can say goodbye, and we can say no.

We believe God cares about our happiness as well as about our growth.

Obviously none of us has reached the full unfolding of love set free—empowered vulnerability. Some aspects may be as yet completely new to us. Empowered loving and living will continually unfold, expand with mystery all our lives, and beyond this life.

There are many metaphors in nature of empowered vulnerability. Mammals, for example, have their soft bodily parts near the surface, with the hard bones deep within, unlike the insects who have the scaly, bony defenses outside. The mammal is immediately aware of the changing temperature, is vulnerable to the challenges of the environment, and learns to respond with the strength of tough flexibility.

The organ of the human skin is exposed, vulnerable, sensitive, and yet powerfully resilient. The very organic cell of which all bodily tissue is formed has a strong, yet permeable cell wall, strong enough to maintain identity and the specific function of the cell yet permeable enough to let nutrients enter from the rest of the body, and for the toxic waste to leave the body.

Another metaphor is that of a deeply rooted, healthy tree,

with roots as deep as the tree is tall, yet with branches open, flexible to wind, rain, sunshine.

Our immune systems are every moment watchfully alert, cleansing, protecting, enabling us to be the open vulnerable creatures we are, exposed to risk and adventure.

God intended us to live both bodily and spiritually in a dangerous world, taking the risks of love, but never intended us to live a life of broken, infected, drained vitality.

> I remind you to rekindle the gift of God
> that is within you . . .
> for God did not give us a spirit of timidity,
> but a spirit of power and love and self-control.
> — 2 Timothy 1:6-7

Both in Isaiah 60 and in Revelation 21 we find metaphors of the strong beauty of the walls and borders of the holy city that God has healed, strengthened, and empowered.

> Your gates shall always be open;
> . . . .
> Instead of bronze I will bring gold,
>   instead of iron I will bring silver;
> instead of wood, bronze,
>   instead of stones, iron. . . .
> you shall call your walls Salvation,
>   and your gates Praise.
> . . . .
> for the LORD will be your everlasting light.
> — Isaiah 60:11, 17-18, 20

> One of the seven angels . . . showed me the holy
>   city Jerusalem coming down out of heaven
>   from God.
> It has the glory of God

and a radiance like a very rare jewel . . .
  clear as crystal.
It has a great, high wall with twelve gates,
  and at the gates twelve angels. . . .
The glory of God is its light. . . .
Its gates will never be shut by day— . . .
People will bring into it the glory and honor
  of the nations . . .
But nothing unclean will enter it.
                    —Revelation 21:10-12, 23-27

In these ancient visions of healed and holy cities, though separated by hundreds of years in their writing, we are shown walls, borders, not built out of defensive fear but as radiant borders of God-empowered, God-illuminated identities.

They can be compared to membranes around healthy body organs, enabling them to work in harmony with other organs, yet to keep their own unique functions. These borders are the living protection which keep out the "uncleanness," yet which are permeable enough for nutrients to enter.

Such borders, it is made clear in both the visions of Isaiah and of John, author of Revelation, are in themselves sources of great beauty and radiance. Isaiah speaks of them as gold and silver, and John compares them to the glowing luster of jewels. At the same time, both speak of the strength and power of these bordering walls that enfold and protect that holy city.

In both visions, the cities are seen as cleansed and empowered by the burning, shining light at their center, God's own self. This intimate, radiant heart re-creates these walls into borders of beauty and enables us to open our gates both to receive and to give. This central glowing light is that which cleanses the city of what does not belong to it, protects it from invasion, and shines not only in it but through it.

This city of God does not exist in some far-off state of perfection, but is implanted within us, here and now, in the very midst of our sins, wounds, and ambiguities.

"See, the home of God is among mortals" (Rev. 21:3).

It is here, God with us. But only rarely do we know it and open to it.

Meditations on Empowered Vulnerability

Meditation One

> They are like trees
>   planted by streams of water,
> which yield their fruit in its season.
>   — Psalm 1:3

Make your whole body comfortable in whatever way is best for you, whether sitting up or lying down. Breathe in and out, slowly, gently, fully, without any pushing, from the soles of your feet to the top of your head. Let the breath flow through you like a quiet river of light. Take as long as you need to feel God's peace.

You may choose to stay with the quiet breathing of the light through your body. But if you feel ready, think of a strong, healthy tree, with roots thrust deep in the earth. Picture the wide interlacing of the roots, like veins and arteries, searching out the underground springs of water, absorbing the moisture and the soil's rich nourishment. The taproot goes deepest of all, down to deeper levels of water. Stay focused on the roots as long as you wish, while they drink.

When ready, picture or just sense the nutrients and moisture flowing higher up the tree, slowly, but fully, into the trunk, the branches, the twigs, the leaves. The whole thirsty tree is drinking in all that it needs.

When you feel ready, think of those wide-spreading, stretching branches. They stretch into the air as high as the roots stretch deep into the earth. See the leaves receiving the particles of gold sunlight. Let the golden light flow through each leaf, each twig, down through the branches, the tree trunk, and into the roots. Let every tiny root be filled with the power of the sunlight.

Stay with this image as long as you wish. When ready, sense or picture the sunlight from the leaves and the moisture from the earth mingling together, flowing with quiet power throughout the whole tree.

If there is anything that is not right for the tree, infection, insect invasion, dark spots, let it go out of the tree, down through the tap-root, deep into the ground, down to the very center of the earth. You do not need to know necessarily what it is that is being sent out of the tree. It is enough to know that the tree is being cleansed of what does not belong to it.

Rest yourself in this picture as long as you wish. Think of yourself *as* this strong, flexible tree. As you breathe each gentle breath, let the roots go deeper and the branches expand wider. The tree can sway and bend with ease because the roots are so deep and strong. The tree can breathe the world's air because it will be cleansed of what it does not need, what does not belong to it.

> Beloved, gaze in thine own heart,
> The holy tree is growing there;
> From joy the holy branches start,
> And all the trembling flowers they bear.
> The changing colours of its fruit
> Have dowered the stars with merry light;
> The surety of its hidden root
> Has planted quiet in the night.
> — W. B. Yeats, "The Two Trees"

When you feel ready to close your meditation, take a few moments of silence as you prepare for re-entry into your everyday life. In the days to come, often look into your heart at your radiant tree of empowered vulnerability.

Meditation Two

(Either to follow the first meditation, or to be used separately.)

> They need no light of lamp or sun,
> for the Lord God will be their light.
>   — Revelation 22:5

As you relax, breathing gently and fully, sense or picture a river of light (or color) flowing through your body, then around it. Let the light form strong, healthy, living borders around your whole body. Let these borders be as close to your body, or as widely expanded as feels right.

Let these borders breathe as you breathe. Like windows, they let light flow out as well as in. Perhaps you can sense them as wings you can fold around you.

Sit at peace within your shining walls or borders of light. When you feel ready, picture within you the source of these powerful wings or walls of light around you. It flows from your center, the center of your heart. It is God's own living presence and light.

Picture or sense it in any way that is best for you: perhaps a star radiating brighter with each gentle breath you take; perhaps a spring of clear water welling from your center, sparkling and refreshing; perhaps a many-petaled flower slowly but powerfully unfolding in your heart.

This is the place where you and God "join together." It is already within you now, in spite of pain, anger, fear, fatigue, depression. The more you focus on it, think about it, the more it opens, expands within you, cleansing, protecting, renewing you.

This is the power that will melt prison doors of the spirit, that will melt all bondage, will heal all draining. For now, it is enough to sense its presence, look at it inwardly, breathe it, breathe with it, let it breathe through you.

Take all the time you need. When ready, open your eyes and keep a few moments of silence before interacting with others. Keep with you throughout the day the sense of the inner unfolding power of the spring or the flower or the star.

2

A Non-Abusive Approach to Spiritual Recovery and Release

The doors of the house where the disciples had met
were locked for fear. . . .
Jesus came and stood among them and said,
"Peace be with you."

— John 20:19

As we explore the shadowed power of communal wounding and the healing release and recovery, it is vital that the spiritual approach does not in itself wound us further.

It is dangerous to enter these hot, inflamed areas of the personality without the deepest sensitivity and respect for the space, timing, reserves, and defenses of ourselves and others. Obviously, we hope there will be healing of the locked-up defendedness. Rigid, embattled walls of separation are the opposite of the radiant healthy borders on which we meditated in the previous chapter. Nevertheless, the defensive walls grew as a way of survival during our powerlessness. They were a shield for an inner self which was totally vulnerable and which had experienced abuse of trust.

Forceful methods and language have *no* legitimate place when it comes to inner healing of the deep fears and hurts. Spiritual commands such as: kill the ego, break down your walls, tear off your masks, take a leap of faith, give up your control, submit, surrender, are abusive to people who are already deeply wounded at the very heart of their ability to trust.

Recently at a retreat, one of the members shared with us her experience of bathing her dog. The dog had undergone abusive treatment at some earlier point in his life, and he was terrified of water. One day when he was especially muddy, she put him in the tub to wash him while he squirmed and whimpered. Suddenly she knew what she needed to do to heal him of that fear. She got into the tub with him, sat in the muddy water holding him in her arms, stroking and talking to him in a calm voice. Eventually he relaxed enough to let her wash him.

As we listened to this poignant story, I thought of the sensitive doctor who examined our first baby. We were as nervous as she was! He did not pull her away from us for examination when we first entered his office. We sat for awhile with the baby still on our laps while the doctor talked with us, smiled at her, and reached out to hold her hand. Then he examined her eyes, ears, and reflexes while we still held her. Then when we all had relaxed a bit more, he suggested we carry her to the table and hold her hand while he finished the examination.

The gentle building of trust, based on understanding respect for the person's need and timing is the only possible approach when healing walls and wounds.

I remember an appalling night long ago when a group of us college friends sat around in our pajamas in a dorm room, chatting. Ann and Josie (not their real names) were recent friends. Ann became convinced that Josie was hiding some deep pain or problem from us and thus not showing trust in us. Ann set out to pull down these reserves by force. For an hour or two she hacked away, needling, teasing, mocking, shaming, attacking Josie at her most vulnerable points. Suddenly Josie cracked. Sobbing hysterically she poured out not only her own secrets, her own most hidden thoughts and feelings but also secrets of others. I still remember the satisfied gleam in Ann's eyes as she comforted Josie, praising her for giving up her control and surrendering to the group's love. The rest of us sat there hating ourselves for not intervening. We felt as if we had watched a bodily violation. Josie *had* been violated, all in the name of "love."

This is an extreme case, of course. This form of emotional manipulation is both known and practiced in cults and in many forms of ideological training. I have known it to be used only too often in professional training groups and workshops as well as occasionally in group therapy. But even in its mildest forms this practice is abusive of the very trust we are trying to build. I inwardly protest when I hear a retreat or personal growth leader saying: "Follow every point of this meditation. Stick with it, even if it hurts," or "Now turn to your neighbor and share your feelings," or even, "Everyone give the person next to you a back rub!"

These enthusiastic, all-inclusive commands are meant so well, and they are so supremely invasive! No alternatives are offered, or are even permissible. No borders are respected. No gentle unfolding of trust. No free choice. Not even a hint that wounds might lie behind the walls, which should be honored.

Too often, complying with a group's direction is called "surrender to God." It isn't, of course. It is surrender to the group spirit, and there are few things more powerful.

God—the God we see through Jesus—does not force us. Egos are not to be killed but, rather, healed and transformed. Masks are not to be ripped off. The fear beneath them is healed until the mask falls off naturally like a scab off healed flesh. The walls are not to be torn down but healed, perhaps slowly, back into living, permeable borders. As I understand the essence of the Incarnation of God through Jesus, it is grace-filled, with a mighty but gentle power. If we were to look at the dog owner's actions as at a parable, we could say, "The grace of the Incarnation of God through Christ is like the dog owner who got into the bathwater *with* her dog, holding him until he could trust her and the water."

Compulsion can never build this trust, only the love that shares and holds us until the fear melts away.

In one of the most beautiful and powerful Resurrection stories, Jesus comes to his disciples who were hiding behind locked doors because they were afraid (see John 20:19-23). He did not break down the door. Nor, at the other extreme, did he go away offended, or even stand sadly and submissively outside. He respected the door and let it stay closed. But his strong love came through and stood among them. He did not scold them because they were afraid, or tell them they had hurt his feelings and failed in trust. He greeted them with love and peace, and there in the dark, locked room he showed them his wounds in his hands and side. He blessed them and breathed the Holy Spirit upon them, thus empowering them in the midst of their fear.

A week later it happened all over again (see John 20:24-29). *Again* the door was locked and again, while respecting the fact of the door, he stood among them. This time he turned to Thomas, who had doubted the whole thing, and invited Thomas to touch his wounds, first with just a finger if he chose, then with his hand.

I, personally, had an astoundingly similar experience, though I did not see the resemblance until many years later. In my early teens, my beloved grandmother had a heart attack in our home. I woke in the night, hearing the running footsteps, telephone calls, voices, the doctor running up the stairs. Worst of all I could hear the groans of my grandmother in her great pain. She and I had been very close ever since I was born, sharing walks, talks, fun, books, sewing, and drawing. Now I realized that someone very precious was in pain and was slipping away. I was in a total state of shock, I realize now. But at the time I was not aware of any emotion at all. I just felt I had to go away, to hide. So I went into my clothes closet, shut the door firmly, and sat down on my shoes in the dark. Somehow it seemed the logical thing to do. I don't know how long I sat there. I was not crying or praying. I just sat there, not moving. Suddenly, though the door stayed closed, someone was there in the dark closet with me. I neither saw nor heard anything, but the Presence was unmistakable. Then someone took hold of my very cold hands with warmth and strength. It was not so much in my physical hands that I felt the touch, but as if it were my *real* hands within my bodily hands. I was gently pulled to my feet, and I began to feel warm all over. Then I opened the closet door and walked out.

The Presence had come into my place of fear and shock with the same gentle power with which the dog owner got into the water with the dog to hold him, and with which Jesus came through the closed door into the dark fear of the disciples. No rebuke, no shaming, no force, just the transforming Presence.

How different from the approach of a spiritual leader I once knew (who later formed his own cult) who banged his fist on the table and shouted to his startled audience, *"Bloom, damn it!"*

"But will we really change and grow through this gentleness?" I am often earnestly asked at retreats. One woman said desperately, "I have been locked up inside my own prisons for so long. I want to get out, I want to move. I think I *have* to be pushed."

Many of us feel this desperation about stagnation. We want to feel we are going somewhere at last, we want to *feel* something. We want to break through to richer, deeper love and living, no matter what wounds and fears lie within us. I think this is the reason there is so much violence still in much of our spiritual language. We wonder if it is the only way we'll get things moving.

But God has forever renounced force over us. This does not mean that God has renounced power. Rather, it means that God goes to the center, to work with transforming radical love from the inside out. Radical means roots, that part of us which is underground, deep in the earth. Jesus often spoke of the gentle power of the expanding seeds in the ground, and the work of the yeast from within the dough—from the inside out.

Even this gentle, radical work from within does not push us against our free choice, or inflict a timetable on us. I could have pulled away from the hands that enclosed mine. The disciples could have refused to listen, to look, to touch. But the heart that is ready to be healed responds and opens to the warmth of the transforming Presence. For some of us it may be a swift change. For most of us it will be more gradual.

"Christ meets us where we are, but does not leave us there," I heard a wise teacher say many years ago. I have never forgotten it. The love of God through Christ meets us, without condemnation, exactly where we are, and by the very power of that meeting, the transformation begins at the center.

This same radical, inner life spreading from the inside to the outside has great implications for our spiritual disciplines as well as for our healing. Most of us try to use a spiritual discipline that works for someone we admire, or that a spiritual leader has urged upon us. That is, we adopt it from the *outside* and try to make it a vital part of our lives. Sometimes this works, but more often it does not.

For years I tried many methods of prayer life. I would devour books that would tell me how to pray, and with each new suggested technique, I would feel I had finally found the answer. None of them lasted more than a few months at most. Every one of them would eventually go down the drain, drop out of my life, much to my guilt. So I would try to use will power to summon up the enthusiasm and energy I had felt at first, and try my latest method harder. After years it finally dawned on me that I was doing violence to myself, forcing myself into shoes that did not fit me. Slowly I realized that *no* method of spiritual discipline was going to become a deep, permanent part of my life unless it came from within me, from the kind of person I really was. I began to examine and really think about the ways I actually *do* respond to others in my most fulfilling relationships. It occurred to me that these would be the ways I would probably respond best to the ultimate relationship—with God. I began, slowly, to develop my own rhythm of response to God in prayer.

To my surprise, I found it was a very different way than most of the ancient, traditional ways urged on us so often. For example, I discovered that early morning prayer, an hour before breakfast, simply did not work for me. I am not and never have been a morning person; those early morning "watches" at church camps and spiritual retreats did nothing for me. What a relief and release to know that God was also with me at two o'clock in the afternoon and at nine o'clock at night. How freeing to drop those awful early morning struggles! What a relief and release to realize that I am a person who responds far better to a flexible, changeable way of praying through the day on a general basis, but who also likes occasional seasons (such as Lent or Advent) for more structured times of prayer. Nothing will really take root in us, unless it comes out of our own heart's unique relationship with God, though of course we can be helped and enriched by hearing the witness and experience of others in *their* ways of praying.

Even when we are in a group situation which requires some general outside structure, we can still be sensitive to individual needs, giving alternatives, options, permission to withdraw into other forms of prayer, or to change the imagery and symbolism suggested.

For example, with each meditation or guided growth process, a leader can say: "If you feel ready for this . . .," or, "Check inwardly how you are feeling about this . . .," or, "What is your body telling you personally about what we are doing," or, "Stay with this point inwardly as long as you need to . . .," or, "If you would rather stay quietly seated than to . . . talk in groups . . . share your feelings with your neighbor . . . form a circle to dance . . . give each other back rubs . . . get to your feet and stretch like a tree . . . feel free to do so."

We cannot take for granted that most persons feel personally liberated enough to claim personal freedom if the leader has neglected to give it. People are frighteningly obedient (even ministers and religious leaders) when told what to do by someone standing in front.

If you are a member of a group in which these permissions have not been given, learn to say firmly and cheerfully, whenever you wish or need to, "I think I just need to sit quietly at this time," or, "Perhaps later I will feel like talking about my feelings." During an actual guided meditation, if you feel led into a place you do not wish to go, you can inwardly pray: "Living Christ, you are the only authority here. Show me a way to pray that is better for me at this time."

The same is true for spiritual or personal growth books— and that includes *this* book, too! Just because an author you respect has put something into print, that does not mean it is necessarily right for you. The most any spiritual leader or author can do is share his or her witness, experience, and observations. His or her way may never be *your* way. Take what is helpful, with thanks. Lay the rest aside for now.

Small acts of spiritual *dis*obedience can be excellent preparation for the release from destructive communal impact, which this book is about, especially if you have been the victim of emotional or spiritual invasion during your life. This does not mean that you will not learn from others. Certainly, if during the healing meditations of this book you open up levels of deep pain, fear, or confusion, don't try to carry it all alone. Talk with trusted friends. You may need a trained counselor or therapist who will help you recognize deep emotional patterns of response. Alternatives of help should never be *either* prayer *or* medical help, *either* therapy *or* prayer. God's healing reaches us through all these ways, and one way can enrich another. Just be sure that your doctor, therapist, minister, friends, or counselor respects your free identity, discusses options with you, and never tries to take down your defenses by storm or force.

Forceful, abusive forms of spiritual growth, whether we take them from others or inflict them on ourselves, never really change us at the center. The true transformation, the gift of *self-render* (far better than *surrender*) is infinitely more full and rapturous when flowing from the trust that is healed and set free.

Healing Meditation for Inner Fear and Defendedness

The doors of the house where the disciples had met were locked for fear. . . .
Jesus came and stood among them and said, "Peace be with you."

— John 20:19

Make your body comfortable in whatever way is best for you, lying down or sitting. Claim or picture the presence of the Christ. How does this presence come to you? An inner picture? A light? A feeling? Rest in that presence, slowly, gently, fully breathing in and out. Each breath is God's own breath of life. Stay with this as long as you need to. This may be enough for now. If you feel ready, think of some part of you that feels walled-off, frightened, powerless, defensive. Is this manifest somewhere in your body? Maybe in tight abdominal muscles, maybe in tight facial muscles. Check through your body: Where are the defended areas, or the areas that feel too vulnerable, powerless?

What hides behind these doors? some wound of trust? an unhealed memory? an experience of emotional or bodily invasion? a sense of being used and drained by others? Take all the time you need to search yourself in a gentle way. The living Christ near you already knows about this hidden fear and is not angry that you have needed these locked doors.

Perhaps this is as far as you wish to go at this time, which is fine. But if you feel this is a safe place where you can move on, then picture or sense the flowing light of Christ quietly entering your walled-off place. Christ does not break in or tear away the wall. Christ respects your door. But the love and glowing light quietly enter this protected place.

You are not asked to do anything, or to make any surrender. It is enough for you just to look at Christ's light, and let it be near you. If you do wish to reach out and touch, it is enough to use just one finger as Thomas did so long ago.

Quietly rest and breathe. The Christ, the healer, breathes with you, and then says, "Receive the empowerment of God's love, the Holy Spirit."

You don't need to do anything about this. Just hear it, allow it to be said to you, gaze at the light, feel the presence.

Sense or picture the healer walking to your closed door, and laying gentle hands on it. Nothing is forced, but the door is being healed also. You may notice the door changing in some way. But if not, there is no hurry. It will happen when the time is right for you. Rest and breathe the presence of the light as long as you wish.

When you feel ready, move out of meditation, perhaps lightly rubbing your face and hands. Take a few moments of quietness before entering your usual interactions. During the rest of the day, remember that the radical, gentle light still shines within your inner room. The healing is at work in your deep, core self.

3

Signs of Communal Bondage and Burden

> And if anyone asks them,
> "What are these wounds on your chest?"
> The answer will be,
> "The wounds I received
> in the house of my friends."
> — Zechariah 13:6

Is there anything more poignant and painful than to realize our deepest wounds have been inflicted by the communal body which nurtured us? Is there anything more bewildering than to realize that the burdens we carry are not just our own, but ones we have inherited or internalized from a loved communal body?

Sooner or later, we will say with Zechariah, "The wounds I received in the house of my friends." What can be done about these ancient and complex burdens of the emotion and spirit of our families, our churches, our nations, our ethnic groups?

Last summer a friend challenged me with this hard question. He is a scholar and researcher within a great ethnic-religious group. He is not a member of this group, but he has closely studied its traditions and writings, and loves this ancient, enriched body. He is also keenly, painfully aware of its ancient shadows and burdens. He reminded me of the Apostle Paul's metaphor of grafting a branch from an unfruitful tree to a more fruitful one, so that the grafted branch takes on the health and strength of the host tree (see Romans 11:17-24).

"However," he pointed out, "the branch *also* takes on any weakness or disease of the host tree. Is it at all possible to love or share deeply with any community, without taking on its darkness, especially if we expect to share its gifts?"

As we begin our exploration of communal infection and burden, it is indeed vitally important to remember the gifts: The deepest shadows are thrown by the highest mountains. Communal bodies that lay upon us the heaviest burdens often confer the richest potential gifts upon us.

Jesus did not spring full grown from God into the world in the way (as ancient myths tell it) that Athena sprang from the head of Zeus! The Gospel of Matthew opens with a long, detailed genealogy of Jesus, showing the generations of the faithful men and women in his ancestry. From this interwoven matrix, God prepared, shaped, and spiritually empowered the radiant Jesus. Every one of our gifts, whether developed or only potential, has been nurtured within the vast, complex interweaving of our human interdependence. It is both the glory and terror of our human condition!

Even within the dark wounds themselves lie hidden the greatest gifts of all. When I think of the story with which this book opened, of the man staring at his reflection in the subway window, I wonder what was the great potential gift underlying the anger that had been passed from parent to child for so many generations. If that energy, now manifesting as infected anger, was healed, what would that power be? a passion for justice? a strength to combat evil abuse? deep power for passionate love? What would this family be like if it were made whole?

I am not saying that there is not evil. On the contrary, our worst evils come from the energy of our potential gifts when that energy has become diseased. But when that sick, but gifted, power is turned inside out, transformed, we see the power in its beauty.

The fire and intensity that made Saul such a dedicated persecutor of the early Christian church, when healed, became the passionate love of the Christ that transformed him into the Apostle Paul: missionary to the world. A healed lion does not become a lamb. It *remains* a lion, but a very changed lion!

If this healing, this transformation has not happened within a communal body, within a relationship, the energy of the potential gift can be awesome in its destructive power, and its shadow over our lives.

This is why personal prayer for our own individual healing so often seems blocked or ineffective. It is because it is not just our own individual history that is involved. In our bodies, our hearts, our personal space, we carry "the devastations of many generations" (Isa. 61:4).

We need deeper, more radical and inclusive praying when it comes to the wounds that did not begin with ourselves and our own personal traumas. We need to become more aware of the communal forces that have shaped and shadowed our lives, as well as the powerful wounds and gifts of the communities *themselves*.

This is powerfully expressed by Walter Wink in "Waging Spiritual Warfare with the Powers," an article written for *Weavings: A Journal of the Christian Spiritual Life*:

> Prayer is not just a two-way transaction. It also involves the great socio-spiritual forces that control so much of reality. . . . These Powers are more than their outer physical manifestations. They also have an inner spirit, a corporate personality, a driving interior dynamism that is incarnated in the outer forms. It is this interiority . . . of institutions that the Bible calls the "angel of a nation" or the "angel of a church." (See Daniel 10; Revelation 2–3.) . . . a genuine, palpable yet invisible force that maintains an institution's ethos despite continuous changes of personnel. . . .
>
> In short, the equation in prayer is not God plus people, but God plus people plus the Powers.[1]

As I read this remarkable article, I thought it could well

apply to the multi-generational personality of a family, as well as to the corporations, nation states, economic systems, political and ecclesiastical hierarchies of which Wink is speaking.

The awareness of the "Powers" that affect and shape us, that en-gift us, and so often dump toxic waste into us is not just a simplistic, self-pitying "blame the ancestors, blame the family, blame the workplace." The implications are far deeper than just who is to blame. We are opened to the passionate compassion of God who longs not only to heal us personally, but who also longs to enter the heart of these communal powers to heal and transform *them*.

In a later chapter ways by which we can pray for communal healing will be suggested. This chapter focuses on our personal release from bondage to a communal sickness, though still intensely aware of the pain of the body around us. There is a profound difference between *sharing* pain and becoming *infected* by the sickness of another. But my friend's question remains, even if God does not require us to share the sickness, is there any way by which we can be released from it?

It is hard, in the first place, to discern that we *do* need release. If we have always lived in toxic emotional surroundings, it is extremely difficult to identify the condition, simply because we have never known any other atmosphere. As far as we know, it is the normal way of life.

My husband Wilhelm was still a small child when the Nazi Party seized power in his country, Germany. He was still in his teens when the war ended, and he can remember only too clearly the psychic emotional darkness saturating the country during those twelve years of his childhood.

"I could hardly remember any other atmosphere," he told me. "As far back as I could recall there was this almost subliminal darkness over and around us all. Since I had lived in it almost all my life, I did not consciously realize it, much less put it into words. Looking back, I can only describe it as hopeless, endless days of rain and fog when the very existence of any sunshine, any other reality, seemed unreal."

I have heard the same remembrances from survivors of dysfunctional families, whether families of outer physical abuse and neglect or the even more subtly devastating emotional, verbal abuse. We hear it from members of families who were emotionally starved, with no warm intimacy. The survivors of these families also speak of the pervasive hopeless shadow saturating their homes, until it became normal for them.

Sometimes we feel this atmospheric condition in certain churches, workplaces, and friendships, not fully realizing our dark burden until we are free from it.

Even people not gifted with clairvoyance often find they are strangely uneasy in certain houses, geographical locations, or even certain countries. They feel somewhat depressed, with lowered vitality. They feel as if the lights had been dimmed, or the oxygen content lowered. They may begin to feel ill if they have to stay in these areas or houses for an extended time, and when they leave they feel as if great weights have been lifted off.

There is no need to ascribe these reactions to ghosts, demons, haunted houses, or ancient curses. It is likely that most of us can discern emotional tragedy or darkness which can saturate surroundings long after the event and which can even create its own reality and generate its own energy. I often wonder if we are affected more seriously than we realize, at deep subconscious levels by widespread ancient sorrows and disasters. For example, child sacrifice was practiced for thousands of years within *many* civilizations around the world. It was considered the best and normal way to placate the gods. Only in comparatively recent times has this practice been challenged. How much does that dark shadow still rest on the subconscious spirit of the human race? Can we be cleansed, free from this ancient stain?

In our own involvement in an emotionally toxic community, there are various signs and symptoms that may help us to identify it. We may feel as if there is a vast emptiness in our center self, a hunger, a need, a longing which never feels quite filled up in spite of personal prayer and loving valida- tion from others in our present relationships. If we feel this way, it is possible that we are feeling the unfilled hunger and need of many generations, still carried around within us.

Another sign is guilt or uneasiness whenever we do have moments of freedom and happiness, as if we were being disloyal or letting others down. If we feel this, we may be trying to make up for the pain of others in our family background.

Another sign may be a sense of burden, a powerlessness, anxiousness, or irritability when going to family reunions, church gatherings, or our workplace. We usually blame ourselves for such a feeling and resolve to do better later, but the feeling returns and becomes chronic. It is quite possible that what we are feeling is not just our own individual problem—but the shadow of a depressed and wounded communal body whose pain has never been identified and healed.

I sometimes wonder if escape dreams (running away from houses that are haunted, on fire, invaded by robbers; fleeing from tidal waves; trying to find one's way out of tunnels or complex buildings or mazes) may for some of us be signs that we feel trapped, pursued, or overwhelmed by communal pain which is older and vaster than that of our personal lives.

How can we tell if we *are* in fact surrounded by communal pain which is affecting and infecting us? What are the signs in the group itself?

It will usually be a group in which pain and trauma are not openly named or freely discussed, at least at their root level. There may be many quarrels, bickering, discussion on the superficial level but the core problem is not addressed.

Or sometimes problems will be discussed in great secrecy with anxious pleas *not* to share this with anyone else: "Above all, *don't* let Aunt Mary [or the employer or a colleague or the minister or the other board members] know that we talked about this!"

Often the communal shadow will be alluded to indirectly through repeated and well-known anecdotes and jokes. Take notice in some family gathering, church meeting, or office party if there is a stinger in the tail of an old joke or story. It makes us feel safer if we touch on deep pain amid laughter. This anecdotal laughter somewhat distances us from the impact of the pain and prevents us from "rocking the boat."

Of significance is a community where there is a high turnover of personnel, members, directors, or ministers; or where there is a high record of illnesses, emotional crises, or inappropriate behavior. It is quite possible that it is not just a series of individuals having individual problems but that these members of the body have become infected by the contagion of the body.

In toxic groups there are likely to be special members singled out as the "troublemakers"—those with addictions, eating disorders, destructive relationships, and other problems. These persons are usually identified by the group as the ones totally responsible for everyone else's pain, the scapegoats. It may well be that these persons act out openly in their lives and habits the unfaced pain of the communal whole body.

It is often a sign of a group problem if the group has no sense of borders, of individual identities, and little or no clearly identified responsibilities. What is one person's business is everybody's business. All thoughts are shared, all letters, all projects, all plans. It is considered offensive, or at least eccentric, if anyone wants privacy or a clearly defined role. In such a "ball of yarn" (as a friend of mine put it) it is more than likely that individual members cannot separate their own feelings and problems from that of the communal body.

At the opposite extreme, if our communal body has high, rigid walls of such strict privacy that there is no warmth or closeness, we can be quite sure that similar, inner walls are being formed within the individual members of the body.

There is nothing new in these observations that have long been noted and discussed by therapists. There are countless excellent books discussing, analyzing, and prescribing for the troubled codependence and contagious pain within communal bodies and their effect on their individual members. But there is still astoundingly little discernment and discussion on the problem within our *spiritualities* as they are usually taught. Liturgies still emphasize sins with little to say about wounds. In books and groups on spiritual healing, much is said about *individual* choices, *personal* mistakes, *personal* faith, changes of *personal* attitudes and actions, *personal* healing—but still far too little about the deep entanglement with the *communal sickness* around us and its profound effects.

"You have cancer because you are repressing your emotions." "You are depressed because you have created this reality for yourself." "You have arthritis because you are an angry person." In such dangerously simplistic diagnoses, I see a very real return to the ancient responses of the so-called "comforters" in the Book of Job, who made it very clear over thirty-seven chapters (before God put them in their place) that "you must have done *something* wrong, Job, or you wouldn't be in this condition!"

I think we are apt to reason this way because it is frightening that illness or disaster may come upon us *not* because of our personal choices, but from complex factors vaster than we are.

Personal choices and mistakes are certainly involved to some extent. But genetic and environmental factors, including the emotional environment we live in, are probably far more involved. Our bodies are truth tellers, yes. But they are telling us far more than what you and I individually have done wrong. They are telling us about toxic air, water, food, soil. They are telling us about chemical additives. They are telling us about genetic vulnerabilities we have inherited. Perhaps, above all, they are telling us about the pressure, stress, burdens, and shadows of our communities; these communities which have so gifted us—and have so infected us.

How can we be released? How can we be healed?

4

Spiritual Release from Communal Bondage and Burden

> Long my imprisoned spirit lay,
> Fast bound in sin and nature's night;
> Thine eye diffused a quickening ray;
> I woke, the dungeon flamed with light;
> My chains fell off, my heart was free,
> I rose, went forth, and followed thee.
> — Charles Wesley, "And Can It Be"

In this radiant old hymn, we are told that the power that releases us is far greater than the power that trapped us.

Not long ago I counseled a young woman who had married a man she loved very much. His family was a deeply shadowed one of many rigid expectations projected on to each other and on to all who entered the family. They were a family of deep hurts over many generations and, as discussed in the previous chapter, these hurts were never openly recognized. Blame was put on the family members who had the more obvious problems, as well as on those who had married into the family. Though there were not many quarrels or open accusations, it was an emotionally abusive situation.

She did not clearly realize what was happening during the first years. She did suffer from a progressive loss of self-esteem and, consequently, felt guilty and diminished. After some therapy for what she had been made to feel were *her* problems, she began to understand how damaged she had been and what a heavy load she had been carrying in her daily living. She had not yet decided whether she could stay with her marriage. Her husband was becoming aware of the harm that was done, both to him and to her. Even so, she was not sure if he was able to experience a radical change in the way he and she would relate to his family. In the meantime, she wanted to experience spiritual release that would set her free at her center.

As she and I worked and prayed together, we realized that seven transitional stages or steps had developed in her unfolding release.

①   The first was the realization that at her center she was *not* a helpless, powerless person. God had created her as a free, empowered spirit. As we shared this faith, I suddenly thought of the words of God to the prophet Jeremiah:

> "Before I formed you in the womb I knew you,
> and before you were born I consecrated you."
> — Jeremiah 1:5

Though Jeremiah was being called as a witness and a prophet, I wonder if these words might be spoken to us all. The soul of each of us is known and loved by God. Surely the soul of each of us has been consecrated (which means designated and empowered) to fulfill the unique task, whether small or great, for which we came into the world. For each of us, that light shines in our central self and the power already exists there, even though we may not know it yet.

②   The second stage was her acceptance of the fact that she *had* been damaged and trapped in this toxic family situation, and that she had not felt free for a long time. This acceptance involved facing fully her very real anger and grieving.

③   Along with this realization came the longing to be set free as a person, whether or not she chose to stay in the relationship. She longed to have her self-esteem healed, to have the burden of hurting generations taken off.

A more difficult step for her was to know that her longing for release was not only possible, but also was what *God wanted* for her. It took her quite a while to know that love, compassion, and sharing did *not* also mean carrying a burden or becoming infected. She began believing in the empowered stance (see chapter one), the love set free. She began using some of the guided imagery. ④

As a fifth unfolding of release, she set limits and borders of what she would and would not accept in the behavior of others towards her. She knew by now that love set free does not mean either submission or surrender. She learned to speak the *full* truth about what she was and what she felt and what she intended to do. Any attempt to pretend to be what she was not put her back into her prison. ⑤

Another important step was to make healthy, dependable contacts with people outside the family. This served her in many ways: a chance to breathe a different emotional atmosphere, a chance to observe how she and others related in a non-abusive situation, and the opportunity for "reality checks" for herself and her situation. At the same time she became intentionally involved in outside, independent activities, projects, and amusements, not only to nurture herself, but to develop more muscle of independent strength. This helped her to know she was not trapped. Finally, she began new ways of praying. Guided meditation helped her visualize Jesus actually setting her free of the burden she had carried so long. ⑥ ⑦

Of course, this process was not really this neat or in this described linear order. Though one step seemed to unfold from the one before it, in actuality her awareness and acceptance hopped around quite spontaneously. It was in looking back that we saw this process of release in all its stages.

The special scriptural prayer we used in her release grew to mean more and more to us as we kept seeing its deepening significance:

Now he was teaching in one of the synagogues
    on the sabbath.
And just then there appeared a woman with a spirit
that had crippled her for eighteen years.
She was bent over and was quite unable
    to stand up straight.
When Jesus saw her, he called her over and said,
"Woman, you are set free from your ailment."
When he laid his hands on her,
immediately she stood up straight and began
    praising God.

                          — Luke 13:10-13

Visiting villages in central Europe, I have sometimes seen women, probably no older than I am, bent over double, unable to stand straight or fully look up. They walk slowly, with difficulty, facing the ground. This may partly be due to inherited, that is to say, genetic, bodily problems or to severe malnutrition in childhood when the bones are still soft and easily formed or mis-formed. Or perhaps as young girls they were made to carry home over long distances huge bundles of firewood, which was usually looked upon as the task of women and girls. Probably such women were often seen on the village streets in Jesus' time.

Whatever the cause, this condition had come upon the woman in Luke's Gospel from causes that were *not* due to her choices or personal mistakes. The passage makes clear that she was not personally responsible for her bodily bondage. Later in the story Jesus refers to the condition. "This woman, a daughter of Abraham whom Satan bound for eighteen long years" (v. 16). That did not mean that she had done evil, but that evil had come upon her. Jesus never taught that illness and tragedy were sent by God or that they were necessarily the results of something wrong we have done. In this case, she had been trapped by *outside* evil.

She had carried this sorrowful burden for many years,

many *long* years, as Jesus compassionately expressed it. By now it had probably become an almost normal way of life for her. After eighteen years of it, her memories of a different life had probably become very dim. She had grown used to this bodily prison and maybe her consciousness of suffering had dulled. The burden had become herself.

It is not clear whether Jesus saw her sitting with the other women in the back of the synagogue, or whether he saw her walking by outside. She must have been some distance away, for he had to call out to her as compassion flooded through him. He interrupted his teaching, called her over, and laid releasing hands on her. This would have been a complete communal scandal, of course: to interrupt the Sabbath worship, to notice a *woman*, and then to call her to come to him, to touch her, and worst of all to do the work of healing on the holy day of rest! Many taboos were being broken! But he was not willing for her to stay one minute longer in her prison, he who had come to set all captives free. Nor was he willing to let her community stay bound by its legalisms one day longer.

Not only did he take the burden off her body, he also released her power and spirit. She stood up straight. I like the translation of this line in *Good News for Modern Man*: "She straightened *herself* up" (TEV; italics mine). She began to praise God, which probably meant her arms were thrown up, her head thrown back, and her eyes raised, a stance she had not been able to take for eighteen years, perhaps half a lifetime. Her *whole* person was released.

What is more, he gave her a name that appears nowhere else in the Bible: "a daughter of Abraham." This was a designation of almost indescribably dignity, of richness of lineage, one that is almost impossible for us to understand. Everyone there listening, however, would have understood its significance.

This jewel of a story appears in only one of the Gospels, but what vast implications it has for us! We see in this story not just a bodily healing but a spiritual and emotional healing as well. We see not only the release of one individual, but the challenge of release for the whole community in its rigid mindset and its deeply ingrained generational prison of the spirit. We see also Jesus' anger and indignation over the communal cruelty that would have kept her bent and burdened one day longer.

We can experience this story not just as an historical event two thousand years ago, but even more so as a radical event offered and happening here and now for us all. I see this woman as a powerful symbol for each of us who is burdened, bent, trapped by generational wounding and communal prisons. I see also the Christ's passionate concern and anger on our behalf, and the intention to release us.

There is an old saying: "I have Jesus in my heart, but grandpa in my bones!" There is much sad truth in that remark for many of us when we see how ineffective religion has been for us, as so often taught. But depth change begins for us when we experience Jesus not *only* in our hearts, but expanding from our hearts and *into* our "bones," and into the full substance of our burdened trapped spirits.

In the healing meditation that follows, I suggest that we identify ourselves with the bent woman, weighed down, molded out of shape by forces outside our selves. The risen Christ is passionately concerned for us, and comes to set us free, no matter what the resistance around us. The risen Christ releases us so we may "straighten ourselves up," to be able to move with freedom and spontaneity, to look around, to see clearly where and who we are, so we may freely decide what we choose to do about our communal relationship.

Remember, you are free to leave this meditation at any moment if you feel anxiety or pain. You may wish to move back into the earlier meditations of this book, focusing upon God's light within you, quietly breathing in and out God's breath of life.

Meditation for Releasing a Long-term Burden

> He (Jesus) stood up to read, . . .
> "The Spirit of the Lord is upon me . . .
> He has sent me to proclaim release to the
>   captives . . .
>   to let the oppressed go free."
> — Luke 4:16, 18

> He placed his hands on her, and at once
> she straightened herself up.
> — Luke 13:13, TEV

Relax your body in whatever way is best for you. Breathe gently, slowly, fully. Think of or sense the presence of the living Christ closely with you. Wait until this seems a safe place for you to be. It does not matter if you cannot *feel* that presence of Christ. It is enough just to think of that presence, or to picture that presence, or to say that name.

Sense your safety in Christ's presence. Take as long a time as you need to feel safe while you quietly rest. Take note of how your body is feeling, its areas of tension and defendedness, the bodily parts that feel unfree or hurting. Let the enfolding tenderness of God through the Christ flow into these areas of body armor and hurt. Let yourself be surrounded with the strong, healthy protection of the loving Light.

When you feel ready, ask yourself in this safe place, the presence of the Christ, if there is a burden on you that you have been carrying a long time, an oppression that has held you down, bent you out of your natural shape by communal powers, generational wounds, constricted you from freedom, from spontaneity. Reflect on this. Have you felt this way all your life? for many years? Does this burden, this prison come from your family, your church, a community you have joined or married into? Does it have its source in some one-to-one relationship?

Try to picture or think of this inner bent-out-of-shape self as if it were a real person you are looking at. How does this part of you look? The burden it carries, how does it look? Remember you are not alone; the Healer is next to you.

Then if you feel ready, sense or picture the Healer speaking to your imprisoned inner self:

"Who are you, beloved? What do you call yourself?" (Let your inner self reply with as much honesty as possible.)

"What has bent you over? What is its name?" (Take as long as you need for your inner self to respond.)

"Would it be frightening to be set free, to be released?" (You may not wish or be able to respond to this yet. You can always come back later. The Healer will not go away or be offended.

"Would you choose to be set free, to love with power and independence, no longer to be afraid, to see clearly, to make choices for yourself?" (Take time to respond from your own center, your honesty.)

"Will you let me put my arms around your burden, your inner prison, and take it from you? Will you let me set you free?"

If you feel ready to consent, sense or picture how the Healer puts healing hands of light under your burden, between your burden and your body, separating it from you. The burden is lifted off, including all its roots which have embedded themselves into your body, heart, and spirit. Perhaps you can picture your burden as a vast ancient plant which has grown into your body, with its interlacing network of roots, now lifted and fully uprooted from you. Your burden is taken fully into the powerful light of God where it will not be destroyed but its energy healed. But it is taken off *you*. You are free of it.

Feel now what it is like to choose to straighten yourself up to your full, natural height. Sense what it is like to breathe fully as you are filled with strength. Sense what it is like to look around you and to see clearly and to act freely. Take time to be with this feeling. Note any changes in your body responses at this point.

The Healer asks you, "Beloved, what is your name now?" (See if a deeper, more powerful name rises within you—a name now given to you by God.)

You may feel ready (or you may wish to take this next step later) to begin to look at your community from your new stance of straightness, truth, and freedom. Do you feel there will be some differences in your relationships now? Will some clear decisions have to be made soon?

When you feel ready, tune in to your body and be aware of what it feels. Focus again on your gentle, slow but full breathing. Bring your meditation to a gentle close, and take some moments of silence before returning to your daily life. You may wish to return to this meditation several times because it may take a while for you to realize fully that there is already within you a straight, strong, shining being, with a deep, powerful new name.

5

Loving without Being Drained

"My sheep hear my voice.
I know them and they follow me. . . .
No one will snatch them out of my hand."
— John 10:27-28

When serving, giving, loving becomes draining and bleeding, we experience a different form of communal toxicity. It can certainly be related to the burden and darkness just discussed, but it is not quite the same thing. It can and does often affect those who are *not* trapped by communal bondage as much as it does those who are. It is more often experienced in a one-to-one relationship than with a communal body as a whole, though there are many exceptions.

I had been working in the ministry of depth healing for several years when a wise, older minister explained what was the matter with me. I had up to then thought a ministry focused on spiritual renewal and healing would automatically fill me with health and energy. On the contrary, I was catching more colds, tired much of the time, and frequently irritable with the people I ought to be loving! It was a disconcerting surprise to discover that I sometimes felt this way when counseling, leading prayer groups, and teaching at retreats.

I had tried to cut back on appointments to make my schedule less crowded. I tried to pay more attention to my limits of time, energy, and emotional reservoirs. This helped, of course, but the basic problem was still there.

I shared this with an older pastor as we ate breakfast

together at a conference. "People are plugging into you," she said, startlingly. "Learn it *now*, that when you are in a position of caring, serving, leading (whether as minister, teacher, or family member) you become a source of life for others at that moment. Lots of people don't know how to take their energy from God, from the general human life around them, and they plug into specific persons. They drain a lot of your energy for their own needs, and, what's more, they deposit in you a lot of their pain." As she talked, the image of a mosquito jumped into my mind, drawing the blood, then depositing the toxin!

"It's nearly always an unconscious process," she went on. "They don't have any idea what they're doing. And it's not usually the *overtly* demanding ones!"

This was certainly a new an most unwelcome thought. Nobody had ever taught me anything like *that* at seminary! Nobody at any time in my life had ever hinted at such a thing. Loss of energy was supposed to be due to illness or inappropriate scheduling. If you felt drained around another person, it was either because they were a selfish, demanding type, or because they somehow triggered uncomfortable associations in you.

I tried to dismiss the idea as pure superstition, with no basis in sensible thinking or in liberal theology. But her words kept coming back, and I had to admit it explained a lot of things that had puzzled me. I was already beginning to learn about the outwardly invisible prisons and darkness of communities that can envelop and infect its members through the generations. Was this invisible draining of strength and vitality any less likely?

Shortly after this talk, a book came my way which explained matters more clearly. This book, written by a respected psychologist, described how those gifted with deep, sensitive perception can actually observe the process by which energy can be drawn from one person into another. This takes place on a level not usually perceptible to our senses except by the symptoms we feel.

The symptoms of course are many and varied. There can be sudden exhaustion, as if all the vitality in our body suddenly drained out of our feet into the ground. (I remember once while leading at a retreat it hit me so hard and suddenly I had to sit down.) There can be sudden dizziness. One can become very cold. We may develop sudden headaches, chilled hands and feet, abdominal tightness and aching, speeded up heart beat. There may be a sudden onset of anxiety, irritability, exasperation. We may feel as if we need more space and air, or we may all of a sudden desperately need a stimulant or something sweet to eat. Eventually there may be noticeable changes in our dreams and unusual symptoms of minor illnesses.

I remember a friend once wrote me that all of a sudden she had begun having nightmares. This was unusual for her. I asked if she had begun any new relationships recently. Yes, she answered, she had recently begun to talk at depth with a troubled woman, trying to give her some religious comfort and guidance. It appeared that she had, without realizing it, either taken on or been "plugged into" by the woman she was helping to the point that she was having many of the same symptoms.

Obviously symptoms should be checked out medically. If no medical causes are found, it may be helpful to talk with a therapist. But if no apparent physical or psychological problem is found, and if these symptoms only occur with certain people and vanish when we are not with those people, it is possible that we are being directly drained of our energy, and that problems are being projected upon us without our conscious awareness that this is happening.

These symptoms of draining and subconscious projection are not necessarily experienced among those who are *outwardly* demanding of our time and energy. Those who drain us in this unconscious way are often quiet, unselfish people who simply do not know how to receive energy from God and the general life around them, and do not know where to put their pain except with the person nearest them.

Unless we understand what is going on, we usually blame

ourselves. We resolve to do better, to be more patient, and the next time it happens again.

I remember a woman I used to know fairly well. She seemed to be a giver, generous with others, enthusiastic, interested. But somehow when I was near her it felt as if there were not enough oxygen for both of us. I felt wilted with her. After long visits when our friendship grew, I developed back pain. The doctor could find nothing wrong. The woman came to me for informal counseling, and though she made no inappropriate demands, I began to experience some of *her* symptoms! I found it hard to separate what *I* felt from what *she* felt. Prayer with her tired me out.

How guilty I felt! Why could I not be more generous and loving with such a fine person? Why did my heart drop when I heard her voice on the phone? Why did I want to hide when I saw her coming down the street? Eventually she moved to another part of the country and we lost touch.

But sometimes after such a connection, we do *not* lose touch, except outwardly. It frequently happens that the need or the influence of a person or group can stay with us, deeply connected in our space, almost like an umbilical cord, through which our energy is still draining. Geographically they are no longer with us—years may have passed since we have seen them—but we have never been quite free or cleansed or their connecting pull on us.

Very different is the glorious connection of the invisible but deep, golden heart rays exchanged between ourselves and those with whom we *choose* to connect. This is the mutual love, nurture, light, blessing, basic goodness of humanity that we can and do exchange with others and that does not drain and deplete us.

The problem with the draining, depleting connection is that it is by no means always experienced with people who we are helping in a professional way, or with occasional friends. It can be happening right in our own homes with spouse, parents, children, brothers, and sisters. The people who drain us may be people we love dearly, even admire, but there is something about them that makes us feel exhausted, chronically irritable, longing to get away at frequent intervals for a change of space and air. Sometimes, of course, there are outer obvious reasons for this, but often it is not an outer demand, but rather that inner drawing on our energy.

It is a problem not easily understood or solved, whether one seeks help through professional service or from a family member or a friend.

In the poignant story of Jesus healing the bleeding woman (Mark 5:25-34) I notice when she touches his cloak quietly there in the crowd, the New Revised Standard Version says: "Immediately aware that power had gone *forth* from him, Jesus turned about . . ." (v. 30, italics mine). This seems to be significantly different from other translations that say: "the power went out of him." There is profound contrast between that which goes *out* of us, and that which flows *forth* from us. The first implies a depleting draining, and the second implies healing energy given from an empowered stance.

The woman's bleeding for twelve years was indeed a depleting, draining process. It not only had drained her body of energy, but also her financial resources. It had made her an untouchable person in her community. But when Jesus' power streamed forth to heal her, he felt it, but there is no indication that he was depleted. In fact, he went right on from there to heal Jairus' daughter.

I've often had to ask myself the hard question: how much my ministry, or any of my relationships, for that matter, was an empowered flowing forth, and how much was an uncontrolled bleeding of energy?

And how much of this energy bleeding was due to outer causes (too many demands, too little setting of realistic borders of time and energy), and how much was due to the hungry needs of others, planted against my knowledge and consent in my energy field, my own space?

It had taken me a long time to learn to come out from

behind my shell and respond in a giving, spontaneous way to other people. It was not that I had been a wounded person, afraid to trust others, but I was born a most reserved person, with a rather low energy level. As a child I didn't want to bother others, but I didn't want them bothering me either. I defended my private space.

But through the years as a fiercely private person, I had learned:

> "The fortified city is solitary,
>   a habitation deserted and forsaken,
>   like the wilderness."
>   — Isaiah 27:10

Once the love of Christ brought me out, I did not want to go back into that fortified city. I didn't want to minister or relate just to *safe* people.

Did I want to become nervous about sharing the pain of others, holding myself detached? And if I *did* claim spiritual protection, did I really want to walk around in some sort of hard, spiritual armor? I wanted to be truly present with others in their pain.

In short, how could I remain open to love, sharing the pain of others, without becoming a spiritual sponge that endlessly absorbs, or a chronically bleeding victim?

Several Biblical stories became extremely helpful to me. A friend who corresponded with me on the subject suggested the story of the four men who carried the paralyzed man to Jesus for healing, even removing part of the roof so the man could be let down right at Jesus' feet (Mark 2:2-5).

This was a helpful picture as we groped for a concept of empowered loving service. His friends did pick him up and carry him for a while. They were obviously compassionately aware of his suffering and carried that in their hearts even as they carried his body, but they did not need to show their solidarity by becoming lame or paralyzed themselves. They gave what they could in caring, compassionate intelligence and paid a real price for it. It is not easy to lift an inert person to the roof on a stretcher, and then lower the weight! They did not try to be the source of healing themselves, but carried him to the true source, the true Healer.

This seems to me to be the main point. We ourselves are not the healer or the source. If we try to become so, or let others treat us as if we were, the desperate draining and fatigue begin. Over a long period of time illness can begin. I have known quite a number of people gifted with healing touch who have become ill themselves with the same illnesses they helped heal. It is not that they were trying to take over the role of the ultimate healer. They were very humble people and ascribed the healing to God. But I think they did not realize how much they were carrying the pain and problems of others around in their own bodies and spirits. I don't think they realized either how many people had fastened onto their own energy fields and drank from them, as if they were the healing source.

What can be done? What spiritual protection can we claim that will shield us from draining and yet not wall us off from others?

"If you be wise, you will make yourselves to be reservoirs rather than conduits" is a saying attributed to Saint Bernard of Clairvaux, who lived almost nine hundred years ago. It is the wisest spiritual guidance I have ever heard.

A conduit is a channel (a word we hear a lot these days). There are two main problems with a channel: It gives out waters as soon as receiving them since it is a go-between, and, if pollution is present, it will flow *into* the channel as the waters irrigate the fields or cities.

Many ministers, caregivers, counselors, healers, spiritual leaders are apt to picture themselves as channels of God, or channels of the Holy Spirit, with the divine energy running from the source, *through* them, the transmitting leader, counselor, healer, out to the world around them or the persons in front of them.

I used to use this inner picture constantly. When I would teach or preach, I would picture the Christ behind me, speaking through me, the transmitter. Or, if I were counseling, I would picture the Christ behind me, speaking or reaching through me to the other. If I touched another in healing prayer it would be with the concept of the Christ again behind me, with the healing energy running through me as a channel, a transmitter.

But through the years I learned the hard way that I the channel would be fastened onto by others as if I were the main source (logical enough, since I was acting as the go-between). And not only would I be quickly drained, but I would also be on the receiving end of the darkness, pain, and problem that they would project into me as the direct channel. For *myself* it was a dangerous inner picture to hold.

A different inner picture or sensing began to grow within me at a Communion service I was leading. As I lifted the cup, broke the bread, and offered them, I felt a subtle, but powerful change. It was no longer the Christ giving *through* me, but rather the Christ giving *for* me. I felt as if my hands were *enfolded*, covered by the hands of the Christ, over and around my hands. I was doing the physical act, but the direct love and healing energy was coming from the hands which enclosed my hands.

Just recently I heard the same experience from a lay woman who at church prayer meetings often anoints the sick and lays hands on them while the whole group prays for their healing. She said as the months went on, she began to feel as if the hands of the Christ surrounded hers and were actually doing the anointing. Since this change has taken place, there have been a number of startling healings occurring in the group.

I think this is especially important for laying on hands for healing, because then the illness of the one we touch does not fasten itself or project itself upon us, but goes directly into the light of the risen Christ.

We are there fully, caring, sharing, intimately participating, but the healing energy does not flow *from* us as a source, or *through* us as a channel, but it flows directly from the light and energy of the Christ that envelops us.

There is nothing new in this. There is repeated witness in Scripture to this dynamic of being surrounded by God, enfolded by God, rather than just obeying God, or acting for God or ever serving God.

> If I take the wings of the morning
> . . . .
> even there your hand shall lead me,
> and your right hand shall hold me fast.
> — Psalm 139:9-10

> For in this tent we groan, longing to be clothed
> with our heavenly dwelling— . . .
> we wish not to be unclothed but to be further
> clothed,
> so that what is mortal may be swallowed up
> by life.
> — 2 Corinthians 5:2, 4

> "Just as the branch cannot bear fruit by itself
> unless it abides in the vine,
> neither can you unless you abide in me. . . .
> abide in my love."
> — John 15:4, 9

We were never meant to try to *imitate* Christ, any more than a fish imitates the water or a bird imitates the air. We are to *abide* in the Christ. For a long time I thought that meant being somehow connected, as if by an electric cord to the energy outlet, the way a light bulb is connected by a cord to the socket. I had an inner picture of my heart connected to that of the Christ by a band of light. I feel now that our hearts are enfolded by the living heart of the Christ, and when the Christ's heart acts, we are there in action too, but surrounded.

This has made a profound difference for me. When I am teaching, counseling, praying for another or with another, there is no "channel" or transmitter present. There is no more category of "drained" and "drainer" present. The risen body of the Christ enfolds me and enfolds the other, and feeds us both. We both need it. We *both* drink from that pool, that reservoir of light.

This is not just a dynamic for mystical experience. It is meant to be an everyday reality. When we write a letter, a lecture, a book, a sermon, we can ask and sense the hands of the Christ covering and guiding ours. When we work in the garden with our hands in the soil or on the plants, the hands of the Christ can enfold our hands. Whether we cook, create art works, touch a restless child, hold a sick or sorrowing friend, the hands and the heart of the Christ enfold our hands and hearts.

In no way does this keep us from the human experience and awareness of being touched, touching, being intimately involved with others. When our hands are enfolded by the Christ, it is not like touching others or the world around us through leather gloves. On the contrary, our human, bodily involvement will be *enhanced!* We feel *more* keenly and deeply the texture, the love, the pain of others and the world around us. Our human-ness is enlarged, not decreased. But now it is a human-ness that is permeated with empowered light.

For me, this has become the meaning of spiritual protection, in which I am *not* detached, surrounded by some hard armor, holding back feelings. We can, within this protection, become more feeling, able to laugh and cry with others even more. We are able to exchange the golden heart rays of love with others with whom we choose to connect. But no longer are we invaded by others or internalizing their problem. When anyone wishes to implant their umbilical cord in us, it is taken instead by the enfolding light of the Christ, and sent to the healing heart of the universe.

It is wise at some point each day, especially after an

intensive interchange with others, to let the light cleanse us of anything implanted and rooted in us. If we believe there is still a connection from the past that pulls at our energy or projects someone else's energy in us, we can picture or sense the empowered light enfolding that invading presence, lifting it out of our body and our personal space, either sending it back from whence it came, or sending it to God's supreme heart. This is a way of praying for others as well as protecting ourselves.

This new experience (it has become for me far more than just a metaphor or picture) has also changed the way I pray for a future event. Instead of picturing the Christ going ahead of me to that future place and experience, healing it and filling it with light, now I picture or sense the light of Christ's risen body enfolding me *and* the future event together, healing both simultaneously.

Many years ago I read Agnes Sanford's witness in her book *Behold Your God*.

> As we become more and more filled with his life, it may come to us to change our prayer and say, "Lord Jesus Christ, receive me into Thy own glorified Being that I may abide in Thee." Words are not great enough to describe that sense of walking about in a body of light that is not our own, but is His light.[2]

I read this passage many years ago, but it took a long time to understand what this meant in an everyday, practical way. I am grateful for this seed put into my heart, which has helped me to understand what it can mean to abide in Christ.

If this picture or sense of being enfolded makes you uncomfortable, do not push yourself into it. You may prefer to think or picture the Christ between you and the person or group you work with, or going ahead of you into a future experience. This too is a powerful way to visualize and pray, and it also shields your strength.

Meditation for Those Who Feel Drained by Others

Even there shall thy hand lead me
and thy right hand shall hold me.
— Psalm 139:10, RSV

Open your meditation by relaxing your body, making yourself comfortable in whatever way is best for you. Breathe gently, fully. This is God's breath of life given to you.

Ask the close presence of God through Christ to make you aware that you are enfolded. You can think of this as a radiant light surrounding you, or a cloak enfolding you. Or you can think of great wings wrapping you round. Or you might picture yourself actually within Christ's risen body of light, at the heart, the center. (Another way of thinking or feeling may be given you that is better for you.) The light that wraps you also shines within your heart.

As you rest in this center, become aware that you are in a safe but dynamic space. You are protected, not walled off. You are open, but cannot be invaded. When you feel ready, ask yourself if someone's need, depression, thirst, emotional hunger has embedded itself in you, maybe long ago, maybe recently. You may sense it like an umbilical cord attached to you, or a vine tendril wound around you, or the roots of a shrub planted in you. It has been sapping your strength and vitality, perhaps for a long time.

When you feel ready, ask the Christ who enfolds you in light to surround that invasion of the past with light, and uproot it thoroughly, gently, firmly. It can be held for a while in the Healer's hands, nurtured and comforted, then sent to the ultimate healing center of the universe, which might look like the gold orb of the sun, or a vast, unfolding white flower. This need that had invaded you, planted itself in you and drained you is now being fed and filled at the source, not in your body and space. This is a powerful intercessory prayer for others.

Sense or picture the Healer covering and restoring the place of the uprooting within you, putting something of beauty in its place, like a fountain or fresh spring, a tree, flowers.

Sense or picture any vital energy of yours that has been drained away returning to you, even if it has been gone for many years. You might sense it as a flock of birds flying back to you, or a crystal stream flowing into you.

If you feel that *you* have planted your need, your umbilical cord, in another and drained that person's energy, picture the other person enfolded by the Christ, the invading cord drawn out and planted in God's own supreme light, like a golden sun. Now your need is being fed from the Source.

Freely choose those with whom you will exchange the powerful heart rays of love like streams of golden light between your hearts.

Sense or picture how the enfolding light, the risen body of the Christ will set healthy, cleansing borders for you, so that you will not be invaded and drained as you give and relate in love to others.

When ready, bring your meditation to a gentle close, taking some moments for silent re-entry before resuming your daily life.

6

Released to Stay or Released to Leave?

The LORD will keep you from all evil;
....
The LORD will keep
   your going out and your coming in
   from this time on.
                    — Psalm 121:7-8

When Jesus healed, cleansed, and released the man of the Gerasenes from the unclean spirits that had so tormented him, the healed man wanted to leave his home and follow Jesus as a disciple. This was understandable for many reasons, of course. Not only was he filled with joy and gratitude to Jesus, but he probably felt quite reluctant to return to his home. After all, they had seen him at his worst and in their fear of him had often had to chain him up!

But Jesus asked him to return: "'Go home to your friends, and tell them how much the Lord has done for you, and what mercy he has shown you'" (Mark 5:19). Strangely, it was different for the blind Bartimaeus Jesus healed later. He *did* follow Jesus after his sight was restored (see Mark 10:52), and thus he left his community.

How will we be guided after some great change has come to us? When I read the stories in scripture about the healing miracles, I always wonder about the *next* day, especially for those who return to or stay in their communities. Did the friends of the former demoniac become nervous again about him, and start looking around for the chains, just in case? When the bent woman was healed and straightened herself up, did she see unmitigated joy in every face? I wonder if the townspeople sometimes felt disconcerted at the change in her. They were glad for her, of course, but what were they going to *do* with her now after such a miracle? She was not always going to find it easy to stay in her hometown.

When we return to our homes, our familiar surroundings, we have changed—but has anyone else changed? Will we feel the pull of the old categories? Though we have learned how to experience protection against the darkness and the old draining, nevertheless, it still exists in our environment, and it is not always easy to maintain the stance of release, love set free.

It took me quite a number of years in the retreat ministry to learn to take seriously the very real problems of re-entry, both for myself and the retreat members. As we walk back through our daily door, we may walk in as a new creation, but the same old creation will be right there to meet us.

Some people returning with the new light, the new joy, are actually driven out emotionally by others. This happened to a blind man Jesus healed: "They answered him, 'You were born entirely in sins, and are you trying to teach us?' And they drove him out" (John 9:34). Jesus himself had to leave his hometown of Nazareth right at the beginning of his ministry, when the people tried to execute him for blasphemy.

The "driving out" might not be a sudden dramatic rejection. Usually it will be an ongoing challenge, or a chronic downgrading of our experience, or a denial or ignoring of what has happened to us. Our new wholeness is (at least on the subconscious level) a threatening challenge to those who prefer to stay fragmented.

Sometimes the problem is not so much a denial or rejection of us personally, but we realize we are in a communal situation in which the darkness and pain are so intense that even within our new light we feel the power of their destructiveness.

I know a young woman who works with abused, deprived young people, those who are runaways, delinquents, in detention homes, or in prison. Not only is she daily exposed to their pain, their aggressiveness and defensiveness, the tough brutality of their speech, and the heart-breaking complexity of their problems, but she is also in an abusive office situation. This young woman has recently experienced some profound spiritual growth and insight. She feels deeply loved by God and has experienced the power of prayer, as well as learning many methods of bodily and spiritual renewal. Also, she really loves her work with her young people and is successful with it. But she is increasingly exhausted, and for the first time in her life, she is experiencing severe, persistent migraine headaches. She wonders if she can keep working in this environment of devastating pain.

I know a man who is married into a family with several generations of depression and alcoholism. His wife has become emotionally and verbally abusive in her own pain. This has become a recurring cycle as her tension mounts. She refuses spiritual healing of depth therapy. Her husband has been set free personally from the shadow and infection, but as he continues to live in this toxic home environment he wonders if he can remain uninfected by the communal sickness. *Can one stay in such a relationship?*

Or what about situations in which one is not so much beset with communal sickness as with deep indifference? Every spiritual leader knows many examples of wives or husbands who have experienced spiritual transformation themselves, but whose spouses are disinterested, blocked off, resistant to any kind of understanding, sharing, or listening. The partner who has undergone the spiritual change feels constantly doused with cold water, and "unequally yoked together with unbelievers," as is pungently expressed in the King James translation (2 Cor. 6:14). Can one keep one's spirit alive in an atmosphere of spiritual mis-mating?

The same problem is often faced by a church member or minister who has experienced great spiritual healing and growth but who meets general indifference, disinterest from the church body. Can one continue to grow and to maintain the stance of love set free in an atmosphere so cold and uncomprehending?

There are also situations in which we have been so firmly fixed in our former categories by the communal mind that we feel ourselves slowly sinking back into the place we were before. The group expectations are too strong for us.

Some of us feel called by God to leave such relationships. Others feel guided and empowered to stay, to return with full intentionality, knowing what they do to that painful relationship, that wounded community. Before we make such a decision, we need clear, careful discernment that this is indeed *our* true cross. Here are some reflection questions when trying to decide:

Is the choice made in freedom, or do I feel pushed and compelled by a mere sense of duty, imitating others, setting a good example to others?

Have I *named* the problem of the relationship or community, seeing it clearly for what it is?

Have I begun to experience deep healing? Do I feel released from the former *infection* of the group burden and shadow?

Do I know how to set borders and limits about what behavior towards me I will not accept? Do I know how to say no, to say stop—and mean it?

Have I learned to listen to and respect my own emotional needs? Am I resolved to tell *the complete truth* about what I feel, who I am, what I need, what I expect at all times? (This is *not* the same as pushing others.)

Have I become capable of loving yet firm confrontation when it is appropriate? "Speaking the truth in love, we must grow up in every way . . . into Christ" (Eph. 4:15).

What is my body signaling? Am I maintaining essential good health and reasonable energy level, or are there increasing symptoms of sickness?

Am I maintaining ongoing body-work, healing of memories, new lifestyles of eating and exercising, and counseling when necessary?

Within the community or relationship is there at least *some* genuine love, some joy, comfort, and honest sharing?

How am I feeling in general about my life? Is there a center of peace and authority? Is there a *basic* happiness and vitality in living?

Are there a number of healthy outside relationships from which I receive emotional support and reality checks? Are there at least a few people whom I trust who are praying for me?

Do I let the Christ enfold me, surround me, go before me to carry the main weight of the cross, and to send the toxic darkness into the heart of God's love?

There will be ups and downs of course, but these questions discern the main central direction and feeling we have about our lives. If we feel a central "yes" to all these questions, it is quite possible that our decision to stay with a relationship may be a genuine cross. *If* and *when* we are guided by God to go into a dark place, miracles can result, we will be sustained, we will know our authentic call to be there, and we will experience central joy and peace in the midst of suffering.

But if any of these signs of a true call are lacking, we must *never* try to summon them up by will power and good resolutions. The fact that they are lacking may well indicate that this situation is *not* our cross, and we are guided *out* of a relationship. This is hard to face for many of us. We long to be part of a miracle of transformation. We long to be loyal, to be part of the healing of others. We feel defeated, guilty, ashamed that we have not been able to bring wholeness to our relationship or community.

The Bible is realistic on all levels. Miracles happen, but separation also happens. Sometimes the intervention, the rescue, the separation *is* the miracle. By one of those divine synchronicities (I increasingly disbelieve in coincidence) I received, a few minutes ago, a phone call from a very fine pastor who shared with me his thought about his Lenten sermon last Sunday. He interprets the biblical call to repentance, which means *turning around*, as including not only the wrongdoer, the abuser, but also the victim, the abused, for staying in the abusive situation. He pointed out that turning around means not only turning away from something, but turning *toward* something. The abuser must turn away from the abusive behavior and toward a positive healed way of life. The abused must turn away from the emotional, spiritual prison and toward new empowerment and self-value.

As we talked, I was remembering a talk I had with a young woman some months ago. She was describing an extremely abusive office situation she was in. "Perhaps God wants me to learn patience," she reflected. "It is much more likely that God longs for you to learn how to be confrontational," I replied.

One of the main problems in this discernment process is the difficulty in recognizing, seeing clearly that we *are* in an emotionally, spiritually destructive situation. In her excellent book *The Verbally Abusive Relationship*, Patricia Evans tells a hair-raising story:

> A scientist conducted an experiment. She put frog number one into a pan of very hot water. The frog jumped right out. Then she placed frog number two in a pan of cool water. This frog didn't jump out. Very gradually the scientist raised the temperature of the water. The frog gradually adapted until it boiled to death. . . .
>
> We are not inclined to notice gradual changes. This is how most partners adapt to verbal abuse. They slowly adapt until, like frog number two,

they are living in an environment which is killing to their spirit.[3]

The same can be said of any form of destructive relationship or commitment, whether family, church, marriage, job, friendship.

In his sermon on the mountain, Jesus gives us a powerful discernment point by which to recognize a situation which is destructive to our spirits:

> "If your eye is healthy,
> your whole body will be full of light;
> but if your eye is unhealthy,
> your whole body will be full of darkness."
>   — Matthew 6:22-23

The biblical meaning of "eye" is the part of us that brings light. If we have entered into any activity, any relationship, intending to receive and give healthy light (love, joy, strength, wholeness), and have discovered that very source of intended light has become a source of darkness to us: "how great is that darkness!" (v. 23)

What are the signs of the creeping darkness, or the increasing heat of the water, to use Evans' example?

We feel a dying of joy, love, strength, freedom, spontaneity.

We feel a growing powerlessness, a sense of hopelessness, of being in a trap, difficulty in making decisions and acting decisively.

There is a drop in our bodily health and vitality, and an increase of symptoms of illness.

We may notice in ourselves addictive behavior that serves as a temporary escape or anesthetic: alcohol, drug use, eating problems, addictive shopping, overworking, excessive exercise, excessive sleep, inappropriate sexual encounters, a lot of escapist reading or TV watching.

We will find it increasingly difficult to tell the truth, the *full* truth, about ourselves, who we are, what we need, what we think and feel. We lie or prevaricate about what we feel because we want to make it easier for others, and to keep a peaceful atmosphere.

There will be growing distrust of one's self, and one's true value and authenticity. We feel unworthy, guilty, responsible for what is going wrong; as if only we will try *harder*, become more loving, work more efficiently, become more attractive, talk more intelligently, all will be well!

We will probably be having symptoms (maybe only in dreams) of restlessness, longing to escape, deep unfilled emotional or spiritual hunger.

There is definitely a growing fear of what others may say, or do, or think about us. We feel a tendency to placate, to be cautious, to smooth things over. We may feel protective towards the very one or ones who are hurting us, because they need "healing and understanding."

Other people, outside this particular community or relationship also notice many of these symptoms in us.

If we, and others whom we trust, notice these signs as increasing realities on a long-term basis, in spite of our prayers and personal growth, it is not that we have failed, but that the communal atmosphere has become so intensely toxic that our inner light cannot remain light. There are times and situations in which no amount of personal healing, counseling, forgiveness, is enough to keep us emotionally or spiritually healthy.

At such times, we must help one another realize that God's call, "Come out," is as *full* of power and promise as is the challenge he gave to the healed man of the Gerasenes: "Go home . . . and tell them. . . ."

In the great complex eighteenth chapter of the Gospel of Matthew, we see much spiritual realism and wisdom about human relationships: those which can be healed and those which cannot. With reference to commitment within a church relationship we find these significant words from Jesus:

"Truly I tell you,
whatever you bind on earth will be
    bound in heaven,
and whatever you loose on earth will be
    loosed in heaven."
                                    — Matthew 18:18

There have been many differing interpretations of what this means. It is my own understanding that it means if we bind ourselves to one another (whether in marriage, church membership, any relational commitment) in good faith, intending to give and receive nurture, mutual love, light, that commitment is honored by God, "bound in heaven." But when the light has become darkness and the bond has to be broken, loosed, that is also honored by God. The decision to make an act of separation in certain circumstances is not only a wise act, but a *holy* act!

It is significant that though the Gospel of Matthew does not tell of the near execution of Jesus in Nazareth as it does in Luke, it does speak of the many "who took offense at him," and that in his hometown area "he could do no deeds of power there" (Mark 6:3-5). These were strong signs that God was guiding him *out* of that community so that he might live fully and might express his empowered ministry elsewhere.

He never left in a spirit of bitterness and revenge. The passage makes clear that sometimes he was surprised and his hopes were wounded, but he did not hate or retaliate when not only Nazareth but other communities rejected him.

On their way they entered a village of the Samari-tans . . . ; but they did not receive him. . . . When his disciples James and John saw it, they said: "Lord, do you want us to command fire to come down from heaven and consume them?" But he turned and rebuked them. Then they went on to another village.
                                    — Luke 9:52-56

It hurts deeply to leave a relationship or group which we have loved, and which we originally entered in hope and joy. It hurts the way it hurts when cutting off an infected part of the body which threatens to destroy the whole body (see Matt. 18:8-9).

Being misunderstood and rejected hurts. Not to be allowed to give what we so long to give hurts, also. It hurts to see a person or group we love left in pain and darkness when we know they could also be released. It not only hurts, it is frightening to pull up roots and leave into an uncertain future. What was in Jesus' face and voice when he left that village that did not receive him and said to his friends: "Foxes have holes, and birds of heaven have nests; but the Son of Man has nowhere to lay his head" (Luke 9:58). He knew all about the pain of the intentional act of separation so that one may live the life that God intended.

It is encouraging that compassionate and serious attention is now given to the affirmation and healing of those who are guided to make an act of separation. For example, some of the mainline churches are beginning to include liturgical prayers for spiritual closure for the separation of a married couple. One such service is found in the *United Methodist Book of Worship*.

God of infinite love and understanding,
pour out your healing Spirit upon *Name*,
  as *he/she* reflects upon the failure of *his/her* marriage
  and makes a new beginning.
Where there is hurt or bitterness,
  grant healing of memories
    and the ability to put behind the things that
    are past.
Where feelings of despair or worthlessness flood in,
  nurture the spirit of hope and confidence

that by your grace tomorrow can be better
than yesterday.
Where *he/she* looks within and discovers faults
that have contributed to the destruction
of the marriage and have hurt other people
grant forgiveness for what is past
and growth in all that makes for new life.
[Heal *children's names*, and help us minister your
healing to *them*.]
We pray for [other] family and friends,
for the healing of their hurts and the acceptance
of new realities.
All this we ask in the name of the One
who sets us free from slavery to the past and
makes all things new,
even Jesus Christ our Savior. **Amen.**[4]

Another such service is found in the *Book of Worship United Church of Christ*. The introduction of this service explains that such liturgical prayers help persons through the pain and trauma of separation, assuring them not only of the continuing presence and prayers of the church community, but even more the continuing tenderness and help of God. As I read the suggested prayers and scriptures, I thought that some such ritual would be helpful for *any* form of intentional separation: leaving a church, leaving a family group, leaving a job commitment of long standing. How deeply healing it would be if at least two or three friends would pray with us:

O God, make us aware of your presence.
You have blessed us in all our moments:
of joining, of relating, of intending, and of
beginning.
Be with us in our times of separating and of ending,

releasing us from those vows we can no longer keep;
we ask in Christ's name.[5]

At the conclusion of the service, there is affirmation given
by the leader or all the community of those attending:

> We affirm you in the new commitments
>   you have made:
> commitments which find you separated
> but still concerned about each other
> and wishing each other goodwill,
> and commitments which help to heal
>   the pain you may feel.
> Count on God's presence;
> trust our support;
> begin anew.[6]

This liturgy combines our basic needs during an act of
separation: the assurance of the continuing guiding tenderness
of God; the naming of the clear intention to leave; the goodwill
of the departure; the presence of responsible communal
support; the challenge to begin anew the life of love set free.

During this process of discernment we must be prepared
for times of painful uncertainty, testing of the waters, trial
separations during which the discernment deepens and
clarifies. Only very rarely can such major decisions be made
overnight. But when the guidance of God becomes clear to us,
whether we return and stay or whether we leave, we will be a
new person, leading a new life. Whether we leave or stay we
will need to be personally freed of the burden and infection.
Whether our cross is one of departure from the former place
and people, or whether our cross is to remain with the former
place and people, *either one* can be safely undertaken only if it
is the Christ's own self who enfolds our hearts and carries the
main weight of that cross.

Meditations

Two suggested meditations follow. One is for those who feel guided to remain in a wounded and wounding community. One is for those who feel guided to separate and depart. Neither meditation may fit your situation at this time, but you may wish to read them and reflect on their possible future significance for you or for someone you know well.

Meditation One: For Those Guided to Remain in Relationship

> You, O LORD, are a shield around me,
>> my glory, and the one who lifts up my head.
>> —Psalm 3:3

Relax your body and breathe slowly, gently, fully. Sense the closeness of the Christ who has healed you and who enfolds you.

When you feel ready, reflect on the woman healed of her bent-ness (see pages 48–50 and Luke 13:10-17). Recall how she "straightened herself up" and how she praised God for her release. Claim again in your heart your own spiritual release and healing that has set you free.

Think of that woman, and imagine how it might have been for her the next day after the healing. She walks through her village, straight and strong, looking around her. If she is at all realistic she knows it will not always be easy to live there in spite of her healed condition, maybe even more *because* of her healed condition.

She has been categorized as the "bent one" for so many years. The villagers are excited now, but as the days go on many may find it hard to live with this new, healed woman. Some people are so used to helping her that they will feel they have lost their role as helpers and comforters! They may, unconsciously, try to put her back in the old category. There may be others who feel threatened or even judged by her new strength and power, as if she felt herself to be better than they. Still others, who may have prayed for her healing for years, now are full of plans and expectations of the way she "ought" to live now as a healed person.

Her old clothes no longer fit her. Many things in her household will have to be changed to fit her new upright stance.

Think now on *your* community or relationship to which you feel called to return. Name as clearly as you can the communal problem that contributed to your unfreedom, your bent-ness, for so many years. Name also, as clearly as you can, the special difficulties you are likely to face. Reflect again on the special discerning points that guided you to return or remain in your community.

Picture the woman walking through the same old streets of her village. But she walks as a new person. She looks at the same people as before, but now she sees them from a whole new perspective. She looks them fully in the eyes, sharing the truth by her glance of what she has become.

What does this mean to you in *your* situation? In a practical way, as well as in your inner spirit, what will it mean to walk straight and tall? What will it mean in your daily life to look *with truth* into the eyes of your community?

She returns to her home and daily tasks, and makes new clothes for herself. How will you make "new clothes" for your new released being? What does this mean for you?

Sometimes she feels the temptation to shrink back and bend over again to make herself less conspicuous and to make it easier for everyone. In what ways will *you* feel this temptation to move back into unfreedom?

Sometimes she feels pushed and trapped by the expectations of others projected on her, as the appropriate ways for her to live as a healed person. In what ways will you be tempted to live up to the expectations of others?

She begins to understand with compassion why others find it hard to live with her newness, but she knows she must stand firm in her freedom. What will best help *you* to love while speaking the truth?

She seeks out the people in her village who will help her to live in her miracle of release on a daily basis, keeping alive in her the spirit of joy and thankfulness. What are *your* plans for finding supportive people who will affirm your freedom and share your thankfulness? Be practical in your reflections.

She remembers when the Hebrew people were released from the land of slavery, "the angel of the Lord" surrounded them with protection, in front of them and behind them, guiding, protecting, as a great pillar of cloud and fire (see Exodus 13:21-22). Though her healer Jesus, in body has left her village, his "angel"—his transforming, strong spirit—enfolds her, behind and before, and she is set free anew each day.

Do you resolve each day in your wounded relationship or in your wounded community, to claim "the angel of the Lord," the power of Christ's spirit, to go ahead of you, behind you, around you, protecting you from toxicity, guiding you, renewing your inner freedom?

> For freedom, Christ has set us free.
> Stand firm, therefore,
> and do not submit again to a yoke of slavery.
> — Galatians 5:1

Meditation Two: For Those Guided to an Act of Separation

> On that day, when evening had come,
> he (Jesus) said to them,
> "Let us go across to the other side."
> And leaving the crowd behind,
> they took him with them in the boat,
> just as he was.
> — Mark 4:35-36

Rest your body and slowly, gently, fully breathe. Claim the closeness of the Christ, in whatever way Christ the healer appears to you in your inner picturing or sensing.

Reflect briefly but clearly the discernment that has come to you that "evening has come" on your committed relationship.

It is Christ's voice that tells you "Let us go across to the other side." Christ does not *send* you, Christ goes *with* you.

Ask yourself if you are ready to make now this inner spiritual act of departure and closure. If you feel ready, move to the point of departure. You can use the picture of a boat (as in this Bible passage). If some other way of departure is better for you, follow what inner pictures, words, or thoughts rise in you.

Inwardly turn to the person or persons from whom you are separating, and give them a farewell blessing in whatever way is right for you. For example, you could say to them, "I leave you in the loving hands of God, even as I am held in the hands of God," or, "May the healing light surround, bless, and enfold you, even as it surrounds, blesses, and enfolds me."

You may wish to make some inner act of separation, such as leaving your shoes, your coat, or a gift on the shore.

It is now the time to "leave the crowd behind." Turn your self away, and go with the Christ to the boat, push off, and get in.

The water widens between you and the shore. You are leaving, you have made that clear act of separation. Look at the boat, look at the Christ with you. Feel yourself as a person who is fully leaving. Take time to sense and experience this feeling.

The Christ is with you there, "just as he is." What does that phrase mean to you at this time?

If you feel there is anything in the boat with you that should be sent back, (some symbolic object), picture yourself laying it in the water so that a wave, a current, a bird, or a fish will take it back to the shore behind you.

Now look ahead. Do you see any shore yet? Or is it still too dark? Do you feel fear, grieving, any inner "storm" rising? Do you feel lonely in the boat in the uncertain dark, with stormy waters and wind around you? Is it hard to see or to feel the presence of the Christ with you? He guided you to this boat, but where is he? Is he sleeping?

Stretch out your inner hands and feel or sense how strongly they are held, even if you cannot see anything clearly. Sense a protecting cloak put around you.

> He . . . rebuked the wind, and said to the sea,
> "Peace! Be still!"
> Then the wind ceased, and there was a great calm.
> — Mark 4:39, RSV

Breathe the center of inner calm. It will be there for you whenever you need it. Look again towards the new shore. Do you feel, see, sense anything special? a sunrise? a bird flying towards you? someone calling you?

The boat touches the new shore. Deep, wide waters now separate and protect you from your former place. You step out of the boat with the Christ. You are surrounded and guided by the one who said to the released Hebrew people so long ago, "I am the LORD your God, who brought you . . . out of the house of slavery" (Exod. 20:2).

Walk into your new spiritual country.

> If I take the wings of the morning
>   and dwell in the uttermost parts of the sea,
> even there thy hand shall lead me,
>   and thy right hand shall hold me.
> — Psalm 139:9-10, RSV

Rest quietly, breathing slowly and fully. The spiritual closure has happened. When you feel ready, open your eyes. Though you are in familiar surroundings, you are in a new place.

7

Spiritual Recovery, Restoration, and Renewal

On a day of salvation I have helped you;
. . . .
saying to the prisoners, "Come out,"
   to those who are in darkness, "Show yourselves."
They shall feed along the ways,
   on all the bare heights shall be their pasture,
they shall not hunger or thirst,
   neither scorching wind nor sun shall strike them
      down,
for he who has pity on them will lead them,
   and by springs of water will you guide them.
                                        — Isaiah 49:8-10

After any release and deep change of body and spirit, it takes longer than we think for *full* healing to take place. The time needed differs between people. But whether swift or gradual, it is a dynamic, unfolding process, one phase growing out of another.

I discern three major stages for full healing: *recovery, restoration,* and *renewal.* They are intertwined, of course, but each has its distinct characteristics. If any are bypassed, not experienced, the healing is not full and complete.

I realized this clearly last year when I had my first experience of major surgery. The process of full healing from the experience became for me a fascinating metaphor for healings on all the levels of body, emotions, and spirit.

The first phase, *recovery,* was the closing of the surgical wound, first in the deep organs and muscles of the body, then the surface layers. In about six weeks I was pronounced medically recovered, wound closed, no infection, pain gone, mobility returned.

But this was just the first stage—as I learned, to my surprise. Now the *restoration* began. To be restored means to be returned to our former self and to the normal healthy condition that we experienced before the medical problem and the surgical intervention. Medically I was recovered, but I still needed a lot of rest because of fatigue, toning up the muscles again with gentle exercise, flushing out the toxic residue of drugs and medication.

Emotional restoration was needed too. I needed to assimilate, to integrate the experience, to recover my inner balance. I needed time to think over the memories of the experience—the strange things, the scary things, the funny things, the mystery of it all. Some memories I could share with others; some would move quietly into my private heart.

Then the *renewal* began. Renewal means to be made fresh. It means a new beginning rather than just returning to the same old ways. As body and spirit recovered and were restored, I began to see more fully the significance of the recent weeks for my whole life. Fresh energy welled up within me. I was learning new ways to live in and with my body, new ways to share what I learned through my ministry.

I was surprised at this deep, complex, many-layered process of full healing. Of course, it wasn't such a neat, uphill progression as it sounds, with each category clearly marked off from the others. It was more like a zig-zag or a spiral progression. I was somewhat indignant that my excellent doctors had not *told* me about the unfolding stages of healing and what one needs at each stage. It would have helped me so much.

Then I thought back to my *own* leadership and guidance of persons wounded in their spirit! For so many years, until I learned better, I led depth healing retreats for inner wounds with very little attention given to what people could expect as their inner healing unfolded after leaving the retreat.

After such a retreat some years ago, a pastor wrote to me. He affirmed the helpful insights given, but told me that some persons at the retreat who had gotten deeply in touch with their pain had not found enough closure for re-entry to their daily lives. "They left the retreat with their gut hanging out and with no one to help them get it back in!"

I took this very seriously indeed. Apparently, I had not even sewn up the wound before they got off the table! I am most grateful to this pastor for helping me see that I was dangerously ignorant of the slow, complex process of *full* healing.

Even when a full healing comes swiftly and miraculously, it still goes through stages even though the process is speeded up. Alexis Carrel, a 1912 Nobel Prize winner, a surgeon, and a writer, was converted to Christianity at Lourdes when he saw a woman's large, unhealed, open sore close and heal in minutes before his eyes. As a surgeon, he noticed even in the midst of his awe-struck amazement that the wound went through the normal stages of healing: deep tissues closing first, blood and discharge drying up, skin healing, scar tissue forming, then skin returning to its normal appearance.

Though Jesus' healings usually included in one powerful impact most of these stages of recovery, restoration, and renewal, there were healings that indicate more completely the existence of those progressive stages.

For example, after he raised Jairus' little daughter from her death-like sleep, he reminded her parents to give her something to eat. She needed full restoration (perhaps after weeks of illness) through nourishment (see Luke 8:40-42; 49-56).

Then there was the blind man who could see again after Jesus touched his eyes, but his sight was not clear and what he saw made no sense: "I can see people, but they look like trees, walking" (Mark 8:24). He needed a second touch, a deeper healing. Jesus touched him again, and at *that* moment he experienced the full restoration of clear, meaningful sight.

Another story told of the cleansing of ten men from leprosy. But only one turned back to thank Jesus and praise God. The others were *cured*, but he who was renewed with joy and thankfulness was made *well*. As I study these and other biblical accounts of full healing, five important needs stand out within the process of recovery, restoration, and renewal. They are not neatly linear, but they all eventually involve: communal support, daily nurture, facing and accepting change and loss, awareness of significant meaning, and inner springs of new life.

Communal Support

We are always and everywhere communal beings. Even in a hermit's cave on a mountaintop, we would still be enveloped, shaped by our early communal experiences. Even if we are guided out of our present relationships, we are still within the shaping forces of some communal environment. Our freedom is not whether or not we will be in community but rather in *which* community.

Our most independent thoughts and actions have been influenced by some form of communal thought, no matter how long ago or far away. We live in a sea of relationships, visible and invisible.

This is why, of course, we can inherit or absorb communal darkness, pain, as well as gifted power. This is why telepathic exchange is not only possible but happens far more frequently and naturally than we realize.

This is how Jesus could go off alone on the lake or the mountain, and yet be as close to suffering human beings as when physically with them. This is how prayer can reach out and act across the miles. Prayer and action are not opposites. Prayer *is* activity. I heard a spiritual leader years ago say that just as a living plant releases oxygen into the atmosphere, so does sincere prayer release new energy into the lifestream around us.

But for full health of body and spirit, it is not enough to live in this *general* communal sea of thought and energy. We all need warm human contact. Repeatedly in medical studies it has been proved that babies will not thrive, will often dwindle and die, if deprived of warm, bodily touch. Victims of stroke, cancer, heart disease, and other serious medical conditions remain in better physical condition and live longer if they have warm, caring relationships.

All caregivers, whether medical or spiritual, should find out if those for whom they care have at least some close emotional relationships when beginning medical treatment and/or depth spiritual healing.

When we are released from destructive communal burdens and infection, and when our emotional, spiritual draining has been stopped, we will certainly need caring, supportive relationships whether we have chosen to stay or to leave a former relationship. We will need supportive relationships with people we like and trust, people we can have fun with, people we can pray with, people who help us be honest with ourselves, people who open new doors to us.

If we have been guided to leave a relationship, we will probably need to wait awhile before making new commitments. We tend to repeat old mistakes. Before new, permanent commitments are made, we need time for the understanding to deepen, to learn to see more clearly.

In time, we will find that we are ready to graft on to a new communal body. In chapter three, I referred to Paul's letter to the new church in Rome. In it Paul compared the church to a branch taken from an unproductive tree growing in the wild and grafted on to another more fruitful tree "to share the rich root" (Rom. 11:17). This was an important assurance given to the Romans as they broke away from their pagan roots. They needed to know they were not alone, adrift, with no longer an ancient communal grounding. They were grafted on to Israel's rich, ancient covenant with God. They had now a new spiritual bloodline, a new spiritual inheritance.

I know of a young man, deeply abused by his own father, who grew to love his stepfather, a man who tenderly loved and nurtured him. He decided to "graft on" to the stepfather's family, taking his name, becoming part of his line. He feels that his new communal inheritance, his new spiritual bloodline is far more powerful in his new life than was his physical inheritance.

Sustenance and Nurture

The words of the Communion service "Take, eat" became a sacramental reality for me during my convalescence from surgery. With more intentionality than ever before, I let God feed and nurture me in many small, daily ways. Even before the surgery I took in God's nurture through all my five senses: listening to music; picturing, sensing the healing light of God flowing through me; gazing for a while at something beautiful several times a day (a small blue flower, a tree rocking in the wind, the sun shining through green leaves). I would walk right into the branches of an anise shrub, breathing its clean, energizing scent. I tried to taste the texture of all my food, not just eat it. I enjoyed feeling the texture of cloth, of a rock, a leaf, of the earth itself. I let my daughter give me the first massage of my life. In our culture we are starved for warm, healthy touch. Does the compulsion towards abusive touch grow, at least partly, out of that long-term deprivation?

We need to touch our own bodies too. We need to lay our own hands on our hurting, stressed body parts: our over-worked eyes, hands, arms, legs. We can gently massage our faces, hands, feet. We can embrace ourselves. These are acts of joy, acts of delight that prolong life, enrich life's quality, and that also accelerate healing on all levels. These are acts of prayer and spiritual response to God's love.

These acts of accepting God's rich gifts in small, daily ways are so essential not just after bodily illness, during bodily recovery, but even *more so* during and after emotional trauma and recovery. I remember well how surprised I was many years ago after a painful emotional loss, how deeply important and significant were the nurturing *little* things. They stood out like stars in the dark night, like spring blossoms in a desert. I was unspeakably grateful for each one of them, so tiny and yet so vast.

I have learned that a vitally important part of nurturing sustenance is to take back our lost emotional, psychic energy. This is especially essential if we have undergone a long period of being drained within a toxic relationship. I once heard this pictured as if we called back to us a flock of birds. Or we could picture a golden, magnetic sun gathering up all that belongs to us that has been drained from us or that we have given away, returning it to us in a golden shower. You may find other ways of claiming and picturing the return of your lost energy. This does *not* mean that we are necessarily withdrawing our love from the persons who drained us. We can still exchange the rays of love from our hearts. But it means that we reclaim the personal strength we lost during the relationship, even if it was many years ago.

Some years ago I heard a powerful prayer of inner cleansing and restoration of energy, attributed to the Navajo Nation:

> My feet are restored to me.
> My legs are restored to me.
> My body is restored to me.
> My mind is restored to me.
> The dust of my feet is restored to me.
> My spittle is restored to me.
> The hairs of my head are restored to me.
> My voice is restored in beauty.
> All things around me are restored in beauty.
> It is finished in beauty.
> It is finished in beauty.

What would these powerful metaphors of full inner restoration mean for you, in your life and your reclaimed energies?

Facing and Accepting Change and Loss

After any radical change, whether of body or emotions, we need time, space, and a sense of safety for inner truth telling. Things have changed. There have been gains, new growth, doors opening. But there have also been real losses, goodbyes, doors closing.

In medical treatment we may have lost bodily organs. We may have had to give up old ways of eating, drinking, or other accustomed ways of living. In our emotional, spiritual healing there may have been real losses: a family circle, a marriage, a friendship, a church, a job, an ideology, a change in priorities, former ways of interacting and responding to others.

We need time to accept and to integrate these major changes and losses.

Eventually, the question of forgiveness will arise. Forgiveness cannot be safely urged during the first stages of healing. First we need to feel safe, to let the pain subside. To tell an abuse victim to understand, to feel compassion for, to forgive the abuser immediately—is abuse all over again!

The best definition I have heard of forgiveness is "to release the other from our expectations." This is close to the ancient biblical meaning also: to cancel out a debt that is owed. This can be done *outwardly* even in the early stages of healing by giving up thoughts of revenge. On the emotional level, however, it can be done only after we have faced the injustice of the abuse and our pain and anger over it. Eventually, the emotional forgiveness will begin to be a possibility. To release the other person from our expectations means that we no longer expect a repayment of what was our rightful due from them.

I knew a man who had not been given a sense of warm intimacy and acceptance as a child. For a long time he carried around unconsciously within him that little hungry child, looking for a father or mother in his friends, his wife, his employer, his colleagues, his minister, his doctor. He was constantly grieved or angry when the parental nurture he sought was not forthcoming.

Eventually, he was able to understand what he was feeling, and was able to accept the fact that he had suffered a severe deprivation. Something essential had been withheld, and harm had been done. There was a long period when he needed to let himself feel anger over this, which eventually evolved into grief that things had had to be that way. After a while, he also faced the fact that there was no way that deprivation could be "made up" to him by his parents. He allowed God to fill up that empty central place. But he also knew he had to cancel out the old emotional debt he felt his parents owed him. As long as he held onto that demand, he was still *within* the prison with them. He hopes some day there may be a *new*, strong, healthier bond with them, but the old pictures and expectations are gone. This does not mean he will allow himself to be victimized again. He now knows his value, his lovability.

Forgiving ourselves involves the same process. We can make restitution as best we can, but we can't really "make up" for the past. We must learn to release the old assumptions and pictures we had about ourselves. God leads us into the mystery of a new life. What we were has been canceled. Yes, there was real damage, real loss, and we grieve over this. But in God new freedom is given as new life unfolds.

> If anyone is in Christ, there is a new creation: everything old has passed away; see, everything has become new!
>
> — 2 Corinthians 5:17

Awareness of Significant Meaning

A biblical healing miracle always had two purposes: to heal the suffering person (always important to God) and also to make an important point and witness to the community. For example, Jesus' healing of the bent woman was certainly an act of compassion done for *her* but it was also a powerful and dramatic witness to her community that God's healing mercy will not be held back by legalistic barriers, no matter how time- and tradition-honored. This healing work done on the Sabbath scandalized many, but God's love sweeps away and breaks all binding restrictions.

For full healing in our lives, whether of body or spirit, we too need to see the deep significance of our experience— the significance for the community as well as for our personal selves.

This does *not* mean that God purposely sends tragedy and pain to teach us a moral lesson! Does a loving parent kick a child down the stairs to teach the child courage and patience in pain? This hateful theology is contradicted by the whole spirit of the New Testament. Nevertheless, tragedy and pain *do* come in this struggling, groaning creation. Someone has said that God does not send it, nor does God allow it; rather, God *endures* it, as the price of giving us free will. But the point is, given that suffering does come, what is the new growth opening in its midst? What springs of new life are revealed?

A young woman told me of her disastrous engagement. It had become an emotionally abusive relationship, not only with the man but also with his family. Realizing the whirlpool of toxic darkness she was being sucked into, she broke the engagement. It took her a long time to heal, for she had put so much of herself into this relationship.

As her healing deepened, she was eventually able to release the man inwardly from the emotional debt he and his family owed her. But equally significant for her was her clear perception of how much she had depended on others for her sense of identity, how much she had always tried to please others and to conform to others in order to be loved. New doors opened for her as she grew to understand the nature of mature loving. Now the agonizing experience made sense. Now she could see not only the person she had been all her life, but also the released person she *could* be. The whole experience became valuable. It became valuable not only for her personally but for her own family as she matured and for her fulfilling marriage later on. Many close friends grew *with* her.

To my astonishment I actually heard myself saying to my surgeon a few days after the operation, "I wouldn't have missed it!" After she left the room, I asked myself what on earth I had meant by such a fatuous remark. That was the sort of thing one says politely to a host after a party, not when lying in a hospital bed very aware of my stitches!

Was I trying to be polite to doctors? Was I observing silver linings and making the best of things? Was I trying to impress myself with my positive thinking? No, it seemed to come from a much deeper level. I think what suddenly and so surprisingly surfaced was that this experience had opened a new level of life for me that would affect not only me personally but also my ministry.

All my life, as far back as I can remember, I have wanted to be in control of myself. I didn't want to control other people, but I definitely wanted to be in charge of what happened to *me*. Up to a point, this is a good thing. We should be essentially in charge of our lives. That is a lot of what this book is about. But sometimes this need becomes a rigid resistance to the deeper experiences that can come when we trust the mystery of living and let it carry us. All my life I have struggled with this paradox, this polarity, this dance in which one knows when to take control and when to release control. It is like enjoying deep water: Sometimes we vigorously swim; sometimes we release control and let the water hold and play with us. Both acts involve trust in one's self as well as trust in the buoyancy of water.

My surgical experience was a challenge from this

fascinating, difficult paradox. Up to a point, it had been appropriate to assume control: choosing a good doctor, reading up on the problem and procedure, making important decisions, actively getting myself in good shape for the surgery. But then there came the hour in which I needed to release, to trust, to allow myself to be carried by the mystery. This release opened for me again new, ecstatic levels of the "dance."

In the poignant story of the walk to Emmaus (Luke 24:13-35), two grieving disciples of Jesus are joined by a stranger as they walk. They share with him their pain and bewilderment that Jesus was crucified. Why had this happened? They had thought Jesus was to be the victorious redeemer of them all.

The stranger talks to them. Drawing on scripture he explains why Jesus *as* redeemer had chosen the way of the cross rather than the expected ways of a triumphant military commander. Later that evening, after the disciples have recognized the stranger as the risen Jesus, they look back on the conversation and wonder why they had not recognized him earlier. "Were not our hearts burning within us while he was talking to us on the road?" He had helped them to understand, to find deep significance out of the suffering.

We need to emphasize again that God does not send suffering. God longs more than we do that we be healed and made whole. But when suffering does come, we are enabled by God to transform the pain into indescribable, significant value. Treasure is so often found in our darkest places. This is not just "making the best of it." A deeper mystery is involved than this glibness. Would most of us give up our scars? Jesus shared and showed his wounded hands and side there in the upper room after his resurrection. I believe he did this not just to prove that it was he and not an impostor. I believe he did this so that the disciples (and we) would know once for all that wounds can be transformed from horror into sources of comfort and radiant light. He carried them on his risen body of light. They were not just absorbed and forgotten. They were valuable.

Inner Springs of New Life

As Jesus healed his disciples after the trauma of both their desertion and his death, he took them compassionately through the full unfolding process of recovery, restoration, and renewal. His first resurrection appearances seem more focused on their release from fear and grief. But as the days went on, he stressed increasingly the new power, the new ways they could be released to the world.

For example, when he meets the disciples by the Sea of Tiberias, he lights a fire and cooks breakfast for them: simple, companionable acts they must often have shared before. Then, in one of the most luminous passages of all scripture, he leads Peter gently through the healing of his guilt over his three acts of denial. He takes Peter aside, out of the hearing of the others and asks three times, "Simon son of John, do you love me?" With each opportunity to respond with love, the healing of Peter's shame over the three denials goes deeper. And with each response of Peter, "Yes, Lord, you know that I love you," Jesus leads Peter into the incredible ministry opening before him: "Feed my lambs. . . . Tend my sheep. . . . Feed my sheep" (John 21:15-17). Peter is about to be released to the whole hungry world! With this vision, these springs of new life, his healing is made perfect.

Most of us will not be led into a worldwide ministry (though we may be surprised!). For many of us, our empowered apostolate will be "Return to your home, and declare how much God has done for you" (Luke 8:39).

But for all of us, whether we are released to a worldwide ministry, or are released to return home as a free, empowered person, or sent to some small but special corner of need, it will come true for us as it did for Peter's mother-in-law. When Jesus laid hands on her and healed her of her fever, we are told simply, "She got up and began to serve him" (Matt. 8:15). That was a healing in which the *recovery, restoration, renewal* went through its stages swiftly. With us it will probably take longer. But with us, as with her, the unfolding healing will release in us springs of new life. Our loving, intimate service will be unique, because each of us is unique. It will be life-changing for others because we are changed. It will be a loving service that is not compulsive but releasing, because we are released. Whatever opens before us will be a joyful mystery. It will be healing made perfect.

Three suggested meditations follow, each one illustrating a phase of our healing as it unfolds and deepens. Choose the one that best fits your situation at this time in your recovery, restoration, renewal periods. Read the scripture passage slowly, several times over, seeing and sensing more personal significance for you each time.

Meditation One

Then Jesus . . . came to the tomb.
It was a cave, and a stone was lying against it.
Jesus said, "Take away the stone." . . . So they took
    away the stone. . . .
He cried out with a loud voice, "Lazarus, come out!"
The dead man came out,
his hands and feet bound . . . and his face wrapped
    in a cloth.
Jesus said to them, "Unbind him and let him go."
                                    — John 11:38, 39, 41, 43

Rest. Breathe slowly, gently, fully. Christ the healer is closely with you. You have been brought out of your own cave, your own dark, lifeless prison. But do you feel still unfree? Is something binding you, holding you back? Take awhile to listen to what your body and feelings are telling you. Is some deeper entrapment present? Old expectations from yourself and/or from others? The pull of old associations? Some difficulty in letting go of the past? If you cannot sense it clearly now, ask to be shown in the days ahead. The *community* rolled aside the stone at Lazarus' grave. The *community* unbound him. What relationship, or what community, has helped you be unbound from your prison? How can you be helped in the deeper release you still need?

Reflect quietly, taking what time you need as you breathe gently and fully, giving thanks for the release you have already experienced.

Meditation Two

> He took the blind man by the hand and led him out
> of the village;
> and when he had . . . laid his hands on him,
> he asked him,
> "Can you see anything?"
> And the man looked up and said,
> "I can see people, but they look like trees, walking."
> Then Jesus laid his hands on his eyes again;
> and he looked intently and his sight was restored,
> and he saw everything clearly.
>
> — Mark 8:23-25

Be comfortable and relax. Breathe gently but fully. Claim the closeness of Christ the healer. Reflect on the ways by which you have been touched with healing love. You had felt lost in darkness and confusion. There was so much that was not seen or understood. Now new light fills you in ways you had never dreamed. But there is still some confusion; some things are still very unclear. The new life seems strange and quite bewildering. You are groping for fuller meaning and significance and understanding and clarity.

Ask the Healer for a second touch for full restoration, for whatever you need to deepen and to complete your healing. Rest; open your heart; see what seems to rise within you; if not at once, then within the next few days.

Meditation Three

> He took her by the hand and said . . .
> "Little girl, get up!"
> and immediately the girl got up
> and began to walk about . . .
> He . . . told them to give her something
>   to eat.
> — Mark 5:41-43

Rest as you breathe the healing breath of God, slowly, gently, fully. That breath, that touch has wakened you from the long, death-like sleep of your full self. You have been released from former pain.

You are well. You are stretching, moving about in your new life. But there is still a deep need for sustenance, nurture, as you restore.

Listen to your body. What is it saying about your deepest needs right now? Listen to your heart and your spirit. What is your deepest longing they are bursting to express?

Ask the Healer to show you the food God is giving you through many different ways. What might they be? Can you take and receive them fully and freely without apology? What changes will this make in your daily life, this period of deep nurture and inner food? Be as clear and specific as possible.

Conclude your meditation gently, stretching and gently massaging your hands and face. Know that the Healer is with you as closely as when with Lazarus, the blind man, the little daughter of Jairus. The deeper release, the deeper clarity and meaning, the daily sustenance that you are beginning to feel will continue to unfold.

8

Healing Prayer for Wounded Families, Church, and Community

I love you, Lord Jesus, because of the multitude who
shelter within you and whom, if one clings closely to
you, one can hear with all the other beings murmuring,
praying, weeping.[7]

— Pierre Teilhard de Chardin

A shining sign of restoration and renewal is when we feel
ready to pray for a wounded community that has wounded
us. But this is a readiness that must never be pushed. As with
the forgiveness (discussed in the previous chapter) we may
need a long time of emotional separation first.

"I can't pray for them yet. I don't want any part of me
used for their redemption. They have used me enough." This
brave and honest statement was made to me by a woman who
had undergone severe emotional and spiritual abuse in a
religious cult.

Not only did she need time, and lots of it, to feel safe and
restored, after years of inner anguish and draining, but she
also still felt the energy pull from those still implanted
"umbilical cords" we discussed earlier. Wisely she turned over
to others any intercessory prayer for the communal body that
had damaged her. Even now she cannot bear to read the Bible
or to hear religious language. The leader of the religious cult
had continually used biblical quotes out of context, in a twisted

way, to punish, demean, frighten, and fragment any self-esteem of the members.

As such victims slowly learn to trust God again through the ways of nature, music, art, the love of trustworthy people, it is certainly not their responsibility, maybe for years, to feel they must minister in any way to the communal body which abused them.

I wonder if this, in part, is what the Bible means by that strange image of "a great chasm . . . fixed" (Luke 16:26). It comes from the story of the poor beggar Lazarus who is contemptuously neglected by the rich man on whose threshold Lazarus lies, pleading for food. In the next life, while Lazarus is comforted and healed in Abraham's heart, the rich man, burning now with remorse, begs Abraham to let Lazarus minister to him by bringing him water. Abraham calls the rich man "my child" (thus indicating a continuing bond of love) but says a great chasm is fixed between Lazarus and his abuser.

We may well need this "great chasm" for a long time while our pain and hunger undergo healing, whether we have come from an abusive family, marriage, church, or workplace.

But in the fullness of time, a renewed person will begin to *want* to pray for the former abusive body. This does not crowd out justice or clear awareness of the harm done. It rises from a growing clarity of compassionate understanding that most abusers were themselves victims at one time, unconsciously passing on to others what was done to them out of their unhealed hearts.

The healed, renewed person who has been set free sees this dark pain, the depression, the spiritual prisons developed through the years of toxicity, helplessly passed on from one generation to another.

The released, healed person also sees the empowered, gifted potential of such a group—if it were healed. The very power which was used so hurtfully when transformed, turned inside out, could become a radiant light, as the persecutor Saul became the Apostle Paul.

Out of this vision grows the passion and compassion to leaven the loaf, enlighten the darkness, open the prison doors, and release the imprisoned. This is the same vision and compassion in the description in First Peter of how Jesus "was put to death in the flesh, but made alive in the spirit, in which also he went and made a proclamation to the spirits in prison" (1 Peter 3:18-19).

I used to wonder why Jesus, though he obviously centered his life and his healings around prayer, had so little to say *about* prayer or praying for others. Even the Lord's Prayer does not mention intercessory prayer. One day it suddenly dawned on me what should have been obvious all along, that the *whole* of the Lord's Prayer is both intercessory and communal: *Our Father, . . . give us this day our daily bread, . . . forgive us our debts, . . . deliver us from evil.* The prayer is intercessory in the deepest possible way, in that we are inevitably involved with those for whom we pray. When we pray for the daily bread for all, we are also sharing that need for bread. When we release others from the debtor's prisons, we also are released from that prison. In this prayer there is no polarized "us" and "them." The act of prayer may be (and often should be) done in solitude, but it is never solitary.

It is the risen Christ's own self who is this connecting body of our praying. I remember hearing a religious leader saying many years ago that when we pray the Lord's Prayer (or any prayer in the name of Jesus) we are not so much saying it, as *joining* it, climbing aboard it. For it is the eternal prayer flowing forever between the innermost, ultimate being of God and the earthly manifestation of that God in Jesus.

When we pray in Jesus' name, we are held together in one heart, one hand, with all those for whom we pray, connected with the redemptive light.

> For in him all things in heaven and on earth were created, things visible and invisible, . . . He himself is before all things, and in him all things hold together. . . . For in him all the fullness of God was pleased to dwell.
>
> — Colossians 1:16, 17, 19

Pierre Teilhard de Chardin, French paleontologist, author, spiritual visionary, and Jesuit priest, wrote of a vision he had of the risen Christ (though he expresses it as a friend's vision) that he saw a vibrant atmosphere surrounding the Christ, and a gushing forth of radiant light which filled and extended itself to the outermost realms of this material universe: "delineating a sort of blood stream or nervous system running through the totality of life. *The entire universe was vibrant.*"[8]

These two visions of the risen Christ, separated by nineteen hundred years, show Christ as the connective tissue of all intercessory prayer, the way the circulating blood or the nerve network connects all parts of the body with the power of nurture and communication. As part of that body, when we pray in the name of Jesus, we receive the full impact of that mighty and transforming light.

When we pray for others within that light, the heart of the Christ instantly enfolds our hearts, joins our hearts, and we are taken to the very core of the pain of others, but in a way that will no longer drain or destroy us.

This heart of God through the Christ is not fulfilled until every atom, every cell, every particle, and every person in the universe is awakened, alive, aware, healed, and released to become a transforming particle of life and light for the next part and person, until all, each, everything, responds to the infinite Lover, who is God.

When we enter by prayer through Christ into the dark places of communal pain, such as a family sick for generations with abuse and addictions, it is best if we share this prayer with others, especially with others who have also been set free from the toxicity of that body. This is not always possible. We may not be able to find other members of that particular family who are clearly aware of the generational infection, or who are willing to pray about it. In that case, we can pray with others outside that group, or pray by ourselves if we need to. But prayer, especially of this type, is always more powerful with others.

It is essential to claim the strong presence of the Christ surrounding, enfolding, going ahead of us as we enter this place of dark, communal pain. It does not matter if we do not *feel* the Christ's presence. Claim it anyway, by name. We must *never* try to go into communal pain by ourselves, or take that full impact upon ourselves, especially if it is a wound of many generations that infects our group or family

Meditations for the Healing of a Communal Body

In the following six suggested prayerful meditations, choose the ones that are most appropriate for you and the group for which you pray. They are mostly based on the visionary witness of Isaiah, who always spoke to his wounded but gifted nation in the name of God who had bonded with this communal body in deep love and longing to heal. (Jesus loved the prophet Isaiah, and quoted from him and his vision of the hurting, hurtful, but beloved community.)

The last meditation of the six is one that suggests words or symbolic acts for those who have difficulty in inner picturing. If with any of these prayers you feel at all anxious or reluctant, withdraw at once from that meditation. Use one that is better for you, or just quietly rest in God's light.

Preparation

At the start of whichever meditation you have chosen, relax your body in whatever way is best for you. Claim the closeness of the Risen Christ, around you and enfolding you, for as long as you wish.

Let your body and inner space be cleansed of anything that does not belong to you (you do not need to know what it is) by flowing out of you into the center of the earth. Let cleansing light flow like a river into your body.

Meditation One

> The LORD of hosts . . .
> . . . will destroy on this mountain
>   the shroud that is cast over all peoples,
> . . . .
> he will swallow up death forever.
> — Isaiah 25:6, 7-8

Picture the community for which you are praying, standing in a circle, even if it includes people no longer living in this world.

In the midst of them stands the risen Christ, like a tower of light in the center of the circle. See, or just think of the "shroud" of darkness and pain flowing from the circle directly into the heart, the center of the light that is the Christ. In that heart of light, the dark energy is being sheltered, healed, transformed. Picture, sense, or think of that transforming light flowing radiantly outwardly from the Christ in powerful waves, entering everyone standing in that circle. (You can picture their faces if you wish, but it is not necessary.) Sense the light forming strong borders, a circle *around* the group, as well, for protection.

You can hold this picture as long as feels right for you, or you can come back to it later.

Meditation Two

> As an eagle stirs up its nest,
>   and hovers over its young;
> as it spreads its wings,
> takes them up,
>   and bears them aloft on its pinions.
>   — Deuteronomy 32:11-12

Picture, sense, or just think of the light of the Christ coming down upon and settling on the whole group, covering it like vast, sheltering wings of light. Let the communal group be covered with these wings, these pinions, for as long as seems right. When it feels time, sense or picture the whole communal body carried up on those powerful wings into a stronger sun, a clearer, cleansing light, a vaster view and vision.

Meditation Three

> You shall be called by a new name
>   that the mouth of the LORD will give.
> You shall be a crown of beauty in the
>   hand of the LORD,
>   . . . .
> You shall no more be termed Forsaken,
>   . . . .
>   but you shall be called My Delight Is in Her.
>   — Isaiah 62:2-4

Picture your communal group as if it were one person: a group soul. How does this symbolic person (representing the community) look? How is this person dressed? What sort of expression is one his or her face? What pain is there? What buried gifts and powers?

Picture this group soul, this person encountered by the

living Christ in the same way the bent woman within you was encountered earlier.

The Healer asks: "Who are you, beloved? What do you name yourself?" (What do you inwardly feel the group person answers?)

"What is your wound?" (Take all the time you need to sense the deep answer.)

"Do you have a deep, buried gift?" (Wait in silence for a response. If it does not come now, it may come later. Or it may come forth in symbolic form rather than a clear answer.)

"What do you want me to do for you?" (Take your time to sense a response from the depths, the core of the wound and gift. Do not hurry. If a stated need comes forth, what do you picture or sense the Christ doing for the communal body?)

"I give you a new name now." (Does another, deeper, more authentic name for the communal body rise in your feeling or thinking? Does it come as a word, or in symbolic form?)

You may wish to return to this meditation several times. Each time you may sense a response at a more profound level, coming more from your center.

Meditation Four

> Before they call I will answer,
>   while they are yet speaking I will hear.
> The wolf and the lamb shall feed together,
> . . . .
> They shall not hurt or destroy
>   on all my holy mountain.
> — Isaiah 65:24-25

This meditation was given me some years ago by one of my students. It is powerfully effective and healing. Reflect about whether the group for which you pray was especially wounded by one or two persons, maybe recently or many generations back: an abuser, a molester, an alcoholic, a betrayer, one who could neither give nor receive love. Picture that person (or persons) standing in the midst of the family or group circle.

Picture with them the Healer, the one who puts each person in the circle under strong protection. Also a ring of light surrounds the whole communal body. When ready, the persons in the group raise their hands in blessing and release towards the abuser in the center, from whom the wounding had sprung. The light of their blessing and release flows towards him or her, entering the body beginning at the feet, rising slowly but fully through the whole body. Do you notice any change that you sense in either those blessing and releasing or in the one being blessed?

Meditation Five

> If the root is holy,
> then the branches also are holy.
>   — Romans 11:16

This meditation is similar to the one we used for our individual selves in chapter one. Think of or picture the communal group as if it were a great tree, with wide spreading branches, and a deep intricate underground network of roots. The roots are as deep as the branches are wide. The branches are the communal body as it is now; the roots are former years and generations. What affects the one affects the others.

Ask the Healer, the Christ, to come to the tree and lay healing hands upon the tree at the point where it emerges from the ground. See or sense the radiant light flowing from the Healer's hands down to the deepest roots, filling each tiny tendril, filling the great tap-root. The roots gratefully and thirstily drink in and absorb the rivers of light.

Are there roots that seem sick, breaking off, tangled together? Picture or think of the Healer's hands going down into the ground among the roots (gently, carefully, but with firm strength) separating them, disentangling them, healing them, and moving out disease, growths, invading pests which drain or eat them. Roots breaking off are attached again so they may feel the full strength of the tree. Those that are especially dry are moved near little hidden springs of water in the earth.

When you feel the roots are ready, let the river of light flow up the trunk of the tree, slowly, fully. Let it flow into areas that seem dry or diseased.

The healing light spreads out through the branches: big ones, smaller ones, tiny twigs, leaves, blossoms, fruit.

Now picture the whole tree shining with light in every part. It is becoming a holy tree, giving out fresh oxygen and light to the surrounding atmosphere.

Where do you feel yourself on this tree? as part of the trunk, branches, leaves? Let yourself drink in the new, fresh, healed power of the tree.

This is a meditation especially helpful when praying for *larger* communal bodies, ethnic or national groups, religious denominations, corporations. You yourself will be affected and changed as you pray, as you experience your personal release from toxicity but also your personal connectedness with your larger communal body.

Meditation Six

For those who have difficulty with inner pictures or symbols during meditative prayer, use a form of words, a prayer spoken inwardly or outwardly. You can set up a photo of members of your family, church, or other group, and while looking at the picture, or laying a hand on it, slowly pray the Lord's Prayer, using the name of the group within the prayer: "Thy kingdom come" in (give the name). "Thy will be done" in (give the name).

Or you may wish to use the words from the Book of Revelation while looking at the pictures or thinking about your community:

> (God) will dwell with them as their God;
> they will be his peoples, . . .
> he will wipe every tear from their eyes. . . .
> mourning, and crying and pain will be no more.
> — Revelation 21:3-4

Or some other words of personal blessing and release may form spontaneously within you. Or you may find a special word or phrase in a hymn or a poem, and whenever you think of or pray for your group, use this word or phrase for them.

Or you can lay your photo (it does not need to be a photo of the whole group, of course; it can be single members, or a few together) under a cross or a vase or pot of fresh flowers, or on a sunny windowsill. This is symbolic, of course, of God's surrounding love, ever fresh like the flowers, radiant like the sun, sharing and redeeming all pain as from the cross of Christ.

When concluding the meditation, whichever one you choose, be sure to cleanse your own body and inner space with deep, slow breaths of God's light. Let anything that does not belong to you but which you may have picked up during the prayer flow out of your body into the ground, or directly into the heart of the Christ. Gently massage your hands and face. Spend a few moments of quietness before resuming your daily life. You may wish to wash your face and hands when you finish.

> You shall be like a watered garden,
>   like a spring of water,
>   whose waters never fail.
> Your ancient ruins shall be rebuilt;
>   you shall raise up the foundations of many
>   generations;
> you shall be called the repairer of the breach,
>   the restorer of streets to live in.
> — Isaiah 58:11-12

9

Released Life in a Wounded World

O dwellers in the dust, awake and sing for joy!
For thy dew is a dew of light,
  and on the land of the shades thou wilt let it fall.
— Isaiah 26:19, RSV

Jesus the Christ sets us free. The burden is lifted, the draining stopped, the toxic wound healed. We may have been guided out of a destructive community or relationship and grafted onto a nurturing one.

But behind us, ahead of us, around us we see the whole communal body of this world, of humanity, in its pain.

"I am not asking you to take them out of the world, but I ask you to protect them from the evil one," Jesus prayed for us all the night before he died (John 17:15). Perhaps we may be guided out of our individual communal relationships, but we are not guided out of the suffering body of the world itself.

I think we all realized this as we watched with unbelieving shock on our news stations the agony of Rwanda. We all saw those hundreds of murdered bodies of men, women, and tiny children floating down rivers, red with their blood, jamming and swirling together like logs.

Where was that pillar of fiery light to lead these victims into safety, as the Hebrews were led out of Egypt? (See Exodus 13:21.) Where is that pillar of fire and light to lead *us* out of such a world where such things can happen?

That pillar of fire and light has gone *within* us, to the core of our hearts, to the core of our communal souls, working its radical (root) transformation, from the inside out. *That* is the only change that will last forever.

In the midst of the dark smoke of fear, hatred, agony—a miasma so thick that even the rescuing angels cannot get through to save the innocent bodily—the heart of God through Christ has not only gotten through, but is *already there*, taking the full impact of the pain.

This is not powerlessness. Force is the opposite of true power. It is the ultimate empowered love that is at work, as the seed works in the ground, the yeast within the dough. It is at work in the heart core of everyone of those killers, in every agonized communal body, like great healing hands thrust deep into the substance of our world, slowly re-forming killers into lovers.

This is how the persecutor Saul became the Apostle Paul. This is how the frightened Simon, denying Jesus at his trial, became Saint Peter, the "rock" on which the church was built. This is why Jesus (according to ancient, heartrendingly beautiful tradition) descended to "hell" after his bodily death, not only to open the doors to all the prisoners, but to come for Judas, especially!

This is how the love of God through the Christ deals with all our hells (whether created by ourselves or by others) by entering them, taking the darkness into God's own heart, releasing, healing, until the hells are turned inside out.

In this vision we dimly have of God through Christ at work in the very core of evil, we also begin to have a dim vision of how *we* share in this cosmic re-formation. We are released from our burdens, healed of our draining not *only* to be freed from our personal pain (important though that is to God's heart) but also to become empowered, radiating particles of life within the sick body of humanity.

As indicated before, this does not mean that we rush ahead into the dark core of any community, let alone that of the whole human race! If we try to do this, even with the best resolutions and the most passionate personal zeal, we will be crushed. In our praying, in our redemptive work, we can go into the dark core safely *only* if we are wrapped, enclosed in the heart of God. *That* is for us the pillar of light and cloud that goes before us, around us, and behind us (see Exodus 3:21; 40:34-38). I am not speaking now of our bodily safety (though I believe we are given that too, much more than we realize). Many men and women have released their bodily safety when in love with the special work they are called to do. None of the twelve disciples died in his own bed at home! To them, bodily safety (though they had been many times miraculously rescued during the years) was not the main point at all. It was the triumphant life, the radiant spirit in love with God that was the point.

A book that literally changed my life as a young teenager during World War II was *This Is the Victory* by the great Methodist minister and author Leslie D. Weatherhead. During the war years, during the very worst of the saturation bombing of London, when his own church was struck and burned, he wrote this book on the radiant life and spirit when bonded in love with the risen Jesus Christ.

Though I was safe in America during the war, I had been in Europe during the grim years 1938–1939 as that dark storm was horribly, inexorably gathering. I had seen the blackouts and the barbed wire barriers, had tried on the gas masks, had heard the voice of Adolph Hitler. As a little child, I was terrified in my heart—more of the evil, psychic atmosphere than of any bodily danger. My family and I returned to America just before the storm of war broke. But we saw the newsreels at the movies, saw the places we had loved, including London, with its burning, collapsing buildings and its dying people. Then came this shining book, *This Is the Victory*, out of the very heart of the horror, based on John's words in his letter to the little Christian churches in dark times:

> For whatever is born of God overcomes the world;
> and this is the victory that overcomes the world,
>   our faith.
>
> — 1 John 5:4, RSV

The impact of this book was almost indescribably powerful, not only for blitzed London, but for Christians all over the
world. That was over fifty years ago, but Weatherhead's book
changed life for many of us whose spirits were lit by his strong
witness that one can live as a released and joyful light within
the torn and wounded body of this world when bonded to the
empowered transforming life of Christ.

But this implies a new and special relationship. Eventually
Christians who are released and healed realize this. It is no
longer a relationship of servanthood, submission to authority,
obedience to orders.

"I do not call you servants any longer, because the servant
does not know what the master is doing; but I have called you
friends" (John 15:15). When Jesus named us friends, we were
brought out of mere obedience into intense, warm intimacy.
There is a qualitative change. Yes, we still serve, but now as
lovers serve.

We have been transformed from the realm of authority and
submission into the interwoven, mysterious organic body, in
which love pours and flows from one living part to another.
No longer in the hierarchical, segmented chain of command,
we relate to our God, other people, ourselves from the inside
out; we relate from the inner life as it flows to the outer life.

This organic, flowing relationship was expressed by Jesus
in many metaphors, especially seen in John's Gospel, which
seems to focus more than any of the others on the intense inner
union between the Christ and those who love Christ. As he
said:

"I am the vine, you are the branches.
Those who abide in me and I in them
bear much fruit."
— John 15:5

"The water that I give will become in them
a spring of water gushing up to eternal life."
— John 4:14

"Out of the believer's heart
shall flow rivers of living water."
— John 7:38

At a baptismal service recently, I was deeply impressed when the pastor did not dip his hand into a baptismal font already filled with water. Instead he took a pitcher, lifted his arm high above his head, and *poured* the water into the font, creating a small waterfall. As he poured, he gave us scriptural verses on the water of life as a direct, loving energy from God that blesses and heals and flows from within us, through us, beyond us.

We begin to see our daily acts of love as flowing like a river from our center, and poured out on the dry and needy lands around us. Our actions become not willpower but *released gestures of pouring*, flowing.

When the woman of Bethany came to Jesus and poured precious ointment on his head, it was a *released* gesture of generous love. "She has done a beautiful thing to me," said Jesus to those who were scandalized at such an act.

To do a "beautiful thing" to God in released, responsive love is intended to be the *only* source of the Christian's words and actions. As one of my students once said to me, "The Christian is released from perfectionism to being a lover of life."

This understanding, this release moves us from law into grace, the grace that flows and pours. When Jesus poured water into a basin and washed his disciples' feet, it was not a moralistic lesson. Instead, it was the modeling of the released gesture of warm, spontaneous caring that he envisioned between the members of his living body, the church.

By the inner flowing of the springs of new life, the bonding with Christ, we are released from bleeding and draining for others to the power to pour out for others. To *pour* and to *hemorrhage* are opposites. When the good Samaritan came to the wounded man lying by the road (ignoring the possibility of bandits still lurking around, ignoring the taboos about touching a bleeding person or dead person) he did not start bleeding too as a sign of solidarity. He "went to him, bandaged his wounds, having poured oil and water on them" (Luke 10:34).

Our bodies, too, begin to release to the poured and flowing river of light. Once, standing in a shadowy valley between great mountains, before the sun rose, I thought how perfect in beauty and formation this valley was, but deeply asleep, how lifeless it was until the sun rose over it, flooding it with warm, golden radiance.

Each cell, each organ, each bodily part is like that sleeping valley until the flowing light flooding every part begins to waken our consciousness to the love and intelligence God has implanted in each cell. We learn to lay a loving hand on our bodily areas calling them to awaken to the glory of the indwelling spirit. A prayer I have learned to use when laying hands on myself has been extraordinarily helpful to me:

> Holy Spirit, Lord and giver of life,
> living presence of the Christ,
> enfold, awaken, and release (name bodily part)
> to the deep wisdom and love
> you have implanted there.

During this prayer, I keep my hand gently on this area of my body, and sense the golden light within it opening like a flower, or flowing like a spring.

In the same way exactly, when we want to pray for a part of this world, some aspect of agonized humanity, as a symbolic gesture, we can lay our hands on a picture from that troubled place, or on a map or a globe, and picture or sense the powerful, transforming golden light opening there like a vast flower, or a glowing pool of water.

Or we can picture or think of the whole globe of the earth, held in the hands of the Christ, or put into the heart of the Christ, until the earth body itself glows and unfolds like a flower.

It is astonishing to me how often I forget to open to the inner flowing. Though I have seen it proved countless times in my life, the miracle of living that unfolds when I act from the inner connectedness with the Christ, I so often forget and go back to my willpower, my personal strength and good resolutions. Centuries ago, the prophet Jeremiah saw his beloved community turning away from the source of living water and spoke the sad anguish of God:

> "They have forsaken me,
> the fountain of living waters,
>   and hewed out cisterns for themselves,
> broken cisterns,
>   that can hold no water."
> — Jeremiah 2:13, RSV

Whenever I start hewing out cisterns, wells for myself, I quickly discover that they break and the vital water trickles away. Whenever I use just my personal strength and love, my life stops pouring and becomes a bleeding, even a hemorrhaging!

But if I can take half an hour, or fifteen minutes, or even

five minutes to quietly open to the inner flowing, before I write a chapter, a sermon, a difficult letter, prepare for a class, prepare for a counseling, prepare for a confrontation over the phone or in person, there is an incredible difference. I no longer scrape away at my dry cisterns for a better word, a little inspiration, a more loving spirit, a calm empowerment.

Yesterday, for example, right in the middle of writing this chapter, I forgot it again! A teenage band using amplifiers roared its thumping rock beat through the peaceful neighborhood! Without taking even a minute to turn to the living waters within, the bonding with the living Christ, I steamed off to the telephone. Yes, I was right to complain. It had happened too often before. And yes, I was right to express anger and a firm request for them to stop. But I was *not* right to surrender to anger to the point where my body and voice were shaking with rage! To use the modern phrase, "I gave away a lot of my power" in that interchange. Dry cisterns, bleeding energy! Had I remembered the inner springs, and drawn upon the living waters of Christ, the confrontation would have been one of loving power that would have strengthened me, not force that drained me.

Clear anger can *also* become a released gesture rather than a trap that imprisons me and the other. At another confrontation, I will try to remember to take a few minutes of preparation to picture or sense the life of the vine flowing into the branch. It may be enough just to think of it, picture it, this deep connectedness. Or I might pray with words like these:

> Living Christ, living vine, living water,
> flow with radiant power into my heart,
> into my face, into my hands and feet,
> into my breathing, into my voice.
> Surround me, enfold me;
> and enfold with your light the experience (or person)
> that I go to meet.

Even business meetings can become a released gesture. Not long ago I attended a committee meeting of an ecumenical spiritual center. It was a meeting of several hours, discussing the details of scheduling, financial resources, and administrative tasks, just the sort of work I dread. But this was different. Instead of the usual brief, formal opening prayer that we expect at church meetings, this group opened with five or ten minutes of silent prayer and reflection. Then every half hour, whoever held the clock (a rotated responsibility) would signal the group for five minutes of silent prayer. It was like watching a miracle to see how tension and disagreements would dissolve in that five minutes of silence. The whole discussion would take a different tone, a different slant. Answers to problems almost formed by themselves. Everyone seemed refreshed rather than wilted at the end. I had never realized that a business meeting could be as renewing as a retreat. I went away thinking, *This is the way Christ intended for the church to interrelate.*

Letting go of the past to the miracle of each new moment of unfolding life becomes also a released gesture. This is often hard to do. We want to clutch at the moments of yesterday. We are used to them. Who knows what newness will bring? This is not only the core of the fear of death, but the core of the fear of life, releasing the accustomed patterns for the mystery of the next moment.

I have always loved the words Thomas Wolfe wrote in *You Can't Go Home Again.* These words seem to me to apply not only to the vision of bodily death and the enlarged life that enfolds it, but to the vision of the unfolding daily life:

> "To lose the earth you know, for greater knowing; to lose the life you have, for greater life; to leave the friends you loved, for greater loving; to find a land more kind than home, more large than earth—
> "—Whereon the pillars of this earth are founded, toward which the conscience of the world is tending— a wind is rising, and the rivers flow."[9]

This chapter is already full of suggested short meditations and prayers. For a closing meditation, I am sharing a poem of prayer that formed within me at a difficult transition in my life in which I was challenged to release and trust the mystery. I did not feel so much that I was composing but rather *listening* to what was being said within. When I struggled for the right word, it felt like removing an inner block so I could hear the word or see the image flowing out.

It formed slowly over several weeks, a line here, a verse there, a word, an inner picture, welling up like a spring of water. I would repeat what was given me as an ongoing daily prayer as I went through this challenging experience. Later on, it became an intercession for others.

As I began this book, I realized how deeply this prayer is saturated with the metaphors of the released, poured out love set free and empowered. I share it to be used as meditation, for personal need, for intercession for another person, *and* as visualized prayer for the wounded communal body of this world.

In This Hour

In the full mystery of this hour
deeper than hearing, vaster than sight,
wrapped in your nearness, lifted in power,
Beloved, I drink your healing light.

Deep is my breathing, heart at rest.
Loosed are the tightened knots of dread.
All that will come, comes full and blessed;
Beloved, I eat your living bread.

Each living breath my body takes
floods through the wounds and walls of death.
With song my sleeping spirit wakes;
Beloved, I breathe your healing breath.

Into my heart a radiant sun,
a sea of shining water flows.
Each thirsting cell, filled one by one,
within, throughout my body glows.

Poured from the glory of your gaze,
immortal waves of love released,
renewed within your heart's bright blaze,
were never born, have never ceased.

This hour is gathered into your hands;
deep in your peace my body lies;
strong in your strength my joy stands;
borne on your wings my spirit flies

into that sun that rings me round,
lightness of light, and glowing flame,
into your sea that does not drown,
into your heart that calls my name.

Gloria, Love, supreme, undying,
Gloria, Jesus, dear desire,
Gloria, Spirit, swift wings flying,
bringing the comfort, bringing the fire.

Endnotes

1 Walter Wink, "Waging Spiritual Warfare with the Powers," *Weavings: A Journal of the Christian Spiritual Life* 5, no. 2 (March/April 1990): 34, 35, 37.

2 Agnes Sanford, *Behold Your God* (Shakopee, MN: Macalester Park, 1985), 125.

3 Patricia Evans, *The Verbally Abusive Relationship* (Holbrook, MA: Bob Evans, 1992), 104.

4 Prayer from "Ministry with Persons Going Through Divorce," *The United Methodist Book of Worship* (Nashville: The United Methodist Publishing House, 1992), 626.

5 Prayers from the *Book of Worship, United Church of Christ* (New York, NY: United Church of Christ, Office for Church Life and Leadership, 1986).

6 Ibid., 295.

7 Pierre Teilhard de Chardin, *Hymn of the Universe* (London: William Collins, 1977), 69.

8 Ibid., 41.

9 Thomas Wolfe, *You Can't Go Home Again* (London: William Heinemann, 1947), 600.

About the Author

Flora Slosson Wuellner, an ordained minister in the United Church of Christ, is well known throughout the United States and Europe for her writings and retreat leadership that focus on the inner healing that Christ freely offers. She has been involved in this specialized ministry of spiritual renewal for over twenty-five years.

The Reverend Wuellner was educated at the University of Michigan and at Chicago Theological Seminary. She has previously served pastorates in Wyoming, Idaho, and Chicago. For twelve years she was an adjunct faculty member at Pacific School of Religion, Berkeley, California.

She and her husband, Wilhelm Wuellner (a Lutheran pastor formerly from Germany and a retired professor of New Testament), experience an international and ecumenical marriage that has "greatly broadened and deepened my outlook in theology, faith, and spirituality." Of her faith heritage she writes, "Deeply influential in my life, work, and outlook were my maternal grandfather, who was a Methodist bishop in the Virginia Conference, and my paternal grandmother, who was a prison chaplain for several years in Wyoming in the early 1900s (perhaps the first woman chaplain in the U.S.)."

Among Flora Slosson Wuellner's many popular books are *Prayer, Stress, and Our Inner Wounds*; *Prayer and Our Bodies*; *Prayer, Fear, and Our Powers*; and *Heart of Healing, Heart of Light*. She has also released a cassette of healing meditations, "Depth Healing and Renewal Through Christ."